LONG WAY HOME

LONG WAY HOME

By Ann Marie Etheridge

DEDICATION

To Jessica and Derek,
my constant inspiration.
And to Stella and Lexi,
my hope for the future.

ACKNOWLEDGMENTS:

Without the guidance of my writing critique group, fondly named 'Peeps,' I would still be laboring away at this memoir. Current and former Peeps who helped to make this possible include Beverley Beckley, Marissa Byfield, Jason Kilgore, Margie Nairn, Sheila Nelson, Donovan Reves, and Dean Sartain. Shout-outs to a few specific Peeps: Beverley's scolding may have sometimes brought on dismay, but her passion to help me write my very best has been a constant inspiration. Donovan is a first-rate editor, helping me create the big picture and providing polished, clear writing, which reflects my intent. Margie has been a great cheerleader, while Marissa's knowledge and innate talent provided constant support and inspiration.

I often needed to clarify one of these long-past events or scenarios through discussions with my siblings, whom I love with all my heart. Thank you Kathy, Tom, Ed, Jim, Rosemary, Trish, and Bernadine. We walked this path together, and one powerful outcome has been the strengthening of our bonds. Sweet Kathy has prayed every night that I get this memoir published, while, as the family historian, helped me get dates accurate, and provided both laughter and tears as we discussed certain events. She has reminded me that I omitted THREE of our family's many evictions from these pages . . . but for the sake of my readers, I judged them best left out for the sake of clarity.

"There is no fixing a damaged childhood.
The best you can do is make the sucker float."
- Pat Conroy
The Prince of Tides

LONG WAY HOME

TABLE OF CONTENTS

Chapter 1:

FROM QUEEN STREET TO THE PROJECTS

Today it would be unimaginable that a person with a seventh-grade education could become a police officer. But after graduating from the police academy, my father was sworn in. It was 1952 and I was one year old. My mother told me that he spit-shined his shoes every day and polished every bullet. She learned to iron perfect military creases, as my father was fastidious about his appearance. I remember hearing him hum to himself each day as he performed the ritual of getting ready to walk his beat in the small town of Woodbury, New Jersey.

For the first five years, Officer McCusker did exceptionally well on the force and was frequently recognized with departmental commendations. Handsome, personable, and bright, he was encouraged to complete his high school diploma so that he would be eligible to make sergeant one day.

As Mama tells the story, in 1957 a huge hurricane hit Woodbury. Our house on Queen Street was set far back in the lot and had an enormous, old oak tree halfway between it and the curb. My father's worry about that tree began the series of infractions against the department that eventually cost him his job.

My father was on duty working the midnight shift. The storm was so powerful and destructive that all officers were called in to deal with the many calls for help. As the winds raged, my dad began to worry about his own family, fretting over the tree in our front yard. He feared that it would crash down, and surely smash through the roof into the attic bedroom I shared with my sister, Kathy. He left his post and came home, scooped up my sister and me, woke Mom and the baby, gathered up Tommy and Eddie, and hurried us all into the basement. There we stayed until the storm blew over.

During that time, my father could not be reached on radio and his colleagues feared the worst. They spent precious time searching for a fellow officer who was not, in fact, in peril. Officer McCusker was strongly reprimanded when he told his supervisor that he had gone home to protect his own family. This not only hurt his pride but also tarnished his flawless record. Over the next year, my father's on-the-job performance declined, as the number of his children rose. By this time, there were six children and I was the eldest at the age of seven.

Mom managed the household as best as she could, but on those occasions when she caught the flu or a cold, Dad gave himself permission to stay at home to "help out." He took up drinking beer and even called in sick a few times when he had a hangover.

Every change of shift gave each officer four straight days off. During one of those furloughs, dad began to complain about a sergeant who "had it in" for him. His anger and sense of indignation grew with each beer he consumed.

Not long ago, I spoke with my mother about that day. She told me, "Your father had been drinking for three days. He considered telling the Chief how unfairly he was being treated by his sergeant. He got himself into such a state that he decided to insist that either the sergeant be fired, or he would resign."

Mom paused to take a sip of her tea and nibble on a cookie. I felt myself getting emotional and took more than a sip from my wine glass.

"On the fourth day of drinking, he got up from his chair and said that he was going to take a walk. When he returned, he told me that he had marched into the department and presented his ultimatum. He got his answer on the spot. The Chief told him to sign his resignation form." Mom looked down as she said this and stared into her empty teacup. I waited for her to speak.

There were things I needed to understand. Had there been an identifiable moment when it all just turned bad? Or had it been really gradual, as it felt to me?

"How did you feel when you heard he was fired?"

"How did I feel? Well, I don't remember how I felt, honey. It was so long ago."

"Weren't you upset with him, Mom?"

"I just remember I didn't want to make him feel worse than he already did, Ann Marie. But I do admit I was worried. I'd just had another baby, and wondered how we were going to get by."

What I wanted to ask her was something like, "So the two of you never heard about or considered birth control?" Naturally, I knew all about the Catholic Church's stand on the issue. Yet I also knew that there were plenty of Catholic couples, who did manage to control the number of children they had. I began tapping my finger on the dining room table. But not wanting to accuse or humiliate my mother, I limited my comment to, "So what happened next, Mom?"

"The next day he woke at the usual time to report to work at 8:00 AM. He put on his uniform and left for the station, telling me that everything was going to be okay because he was going to apologize. Fifteen minutes later he returned home. The first thing that I noticed was a blank space on his shirt where his badge used to be. Then I noticed that he didn't have his holster or his gun."

Mom combed her fingers through her hair, and continued, "You know, Annie, I think he regretted that mistake for the rest of his life."

She may not remember how she felt at the time, but all these years later, I can still hear the sadness in her voice as she told the story.

She added, "In those days, two quarts of beer lasted your father a whole week. So that four days of drinking was quite out of character."

I found myself wondering why she still felt the need to make excuses for him. Her years with him were so filled with suffering due to his alcohol dependence, as were mine. But even now, in her eighties, she idealizes these early years of their marriage.

*** *** ***

My dad began working a series of jobs at which he would initially excel, only to ultimately quit or be fired from. This pattern would last the rest of his life. Nothing else provided the salary, recognition, or sense of self-esteem, which he had enjoyed on the police force.

Months after his discharge from the force, I was a few doors down from my house, playing with Elizabeth, one of my buddies from St. Patrick's kindergarten class, when I accidentally learned that all was not well in my household. The milkman drove up, and Lizzie's mother came out with her wallet to pay her bill. The milkman gestured to my house and made a comment to Elizabeth's mother.

"The McCuskers are months behind in their bill again and I'm going to have to stop delivery. Can't expect another good neighbor to pay their bill again like you did. I just . . . "

Elizabeth's mother looked back and forth between the milkman and me and said, "Hush up now." Only then did he put together that I was from the McCusker household. I may have been young, but it was not lost on me that something had happened that I should be very embarrassed about.

Not long thereafter, my parents announced that we would be moving. But my dad said that before we could find a nice place together, he needed to get a good job and save some money. He went on to explain that the family would have to split up for a few weeks and live with different relatives. There were too many of us to live with one family, he said, but it would be only a very short period of time before we would all be together again. Dad made it sound like a vacation and claimed that it would be "fun." He always did have a way of spinning a tale.

As Dad spoke, I watched my Mom struggle to hold back tears. I knew this was not good news, as Dad claimed. I have often reflected back upon that day. At that age, life is a bucket full of emotional dichotomies: happy/sad, satisfied/unsatisfied, safe/fearful, with the beginnings of more evolved emotions such as esteem/shame, and success/failure. And sometimes they amalgamate into impressions, which would be challenging for a very young girl to understand. My emotions in that moment leaned toward shame, failure, and fear, but all that came out of my mouth was, "Dad, I don't want to live with anyone but you!"

My family was divided among three sets of relatives. Kathy and I were sent to my great-grandmother, who lived with her son (my grandfather). Both had been divorced for years and shared a third-floor apartment above a shoe store in Camden. The front door opened onto the main street. They were Ann Marie Cunningham and William Hartman – "Nanny" and "Pop-Pop" to us. Dad took the older boys to Williamstown, New Jersey, to live with his sister, Bernadine. Mom and the youngest, Rosemary, went to her mother in Camden, a few miles from Nanny's place. I was not pleased with anything about this arrangement, especially since Nanny was strict about my eating habits. Although quite accustomed to being punished by my father for not eating all of my dinners, I knew that Nanny was even worse. I imagined sitting at the dinner table each and every night until bedtime.

I was right. Nanny did make me sit at the dinner table, but at least it turned out to be only a few times a week. Shortly after dinner, Nanny and Pop-Pop would walk to the corner "tap room" and be gone for a few hours. While they were out drinking, I got up from the table and Kathy and I would play. When I heard the key in the door, I resumed my seat at the table, but by then it was time for bed anyway.

My kindergarten picture, 1956.

The planned two weeks of separation from my family turned into four months. I think Nanny felt sorry for leaving Kathy and me alone every night, and so she began to take us to the tap room with her.

The first time we went, Pop-Pop went in one door, and we entered through another, which had a flashing sign that read "Ladies Entrance." The room was full of smoke and had a sweet smell. It took a few minutes before my eyes adjusted to the dim light. Everyone greeted Nanny and asked who we were. The lady patrons were all dressed up and wore bright red lipstick. One told me what lovely hair I had, "What with all of those curls and that strawberry blond color," she just knew that I must be Irish. Another lady told Kathy how pretty she was and how sure she was that one day my sister would be a "Miss America." Nanny went to a tiny window and placed her order: beer for herself, orange soda and pretzels for Kathy and me. Everyone was talking and having a good time.

A woman stood up and put a coin in the jukebox. Suddenly I heard the familiar voice of Mario Lanza, my father's favorite singer. Dad played that same record almost every day and sang along while he shaved. This song was *Be My Love*, and Kathy and I both knew all of the words. We sang along quietly at first, but toward the end of the song, I was taken up by the passion of the voice and did not realize that my own voice was getting louder and louder about *my love*.

After Nanny had a couple of pints, she said in a loud voice, "May I have your attention, please! My great-granddaughter, Ann Marie, has a beautiful singing voice. Who would like to hear this little lass sing?" All those tipsy ladies clapped and cheered. Encouraged by this enthusiasm, I first sang "Dear Little One," a tune I had learned in kindergarten, followed by "Too Ra Loo Ra Loo Ral," one of my father's favorites, and ending with "When Irish Eyes Are Smiling." After I'd finished, a lady called me over to her table and gave me some pennies. Then other ladies did the same thing, and one even gave me a nickel!

By the time I sat back down at our table, I had a lot of money, *forty-six cents* in nickels and pennies! I was excited until Kathy asked me if I was going to give her half.

"No. You didn't earn any of it. It's my money."

"Now, don't you go and get on your high horse and be selfish," said Nanny. "You share that money with your sister right now."

So I did. I didn't know what to do with that much money anyway. When we got home, Kathy and I decided to save the money and give it to our parents to help them save up for a new home so we could all live together again. We planned to keep our stash a secret from Mom and Dad until we had enough to rent a house.

On Sundays Kathy and I got to see our family. Once we had accrued what we believed to be a substantial amount of money – *three dollars and twelve cents* – we presented the savings to our parents during one of these visits. Nanny smiled with pride at our selflessness, as did my parents.

"So how did you girls manage to save all of this money?" Dad asked.

With great enthusiasm, Kathy and I told him the whole story, adding that, "On top of making all of this money, Nanny buys us orange soda and pretzels at the tap room!"

Dad looked down at the floor and didn't say a word for a while. Then he snuffed out his cigarette in the ashtray and took a long drink from his beer before he said, "Girls, you two take your brothers and go into the living room to play. I want to talk to Nanny. Close the French doors on your way out."

We did as we were told, but could hear Dad's shouting through the French doors, so Kathy and I took my brothers to Nanny's bedroom. My father raged at my great-grandmother for taking his daughters to a tap room. Insults were exchanged about who was the worse drinker.

Mom came into Nanny's bedroom, holding the baby. She sat on Nanny's huge bed with the rest of the children and me. The boys snuggled into her lap. Then Dad came into the room, closing the door behind him. He was breathing heavily, and his breath smelled like cigarettes. It was quiet for a few minutes, as all of us just sat together on Nanny's bed.

It was Mom who broke the silence telling Kathy and me to get our nightgowns on. Then Dad told us that we were never to go to the tap room with Nanny again. I was plenty upset by this. Singing at the tap room was fun and I got money. But I knew better than to question his decision.

I wanted to ask him if we had enough money yet to get our own place, but Kathy beat me to it.

"When can we all live together again, Dad?"

"Your Mom and I put in an application to live in a place here in Camden called McGuire Gardens. I don't think it will be very long before we hear." Then, they left, and all I could think about was if we were going to be in trouble with Nanny.

She never mentioned the argument, but Kathy and I were never invited back to the tap room with her and Pop-Pop. Again left alone at night, boredom turned our thoughts to things, which had been clearly forbidden to us. Venturing onto the roof was first, but after climbing a few steps on the fire escape that led up there, we turned back. It was too dark and scary.

Pop-Pop had told us that we were not allowed into his room. Feeling bold after our failed roof adventure, I suggested to Kathy that we take a look in there. She agreed. We opened the door, hoping to find something interesting. But it was just a regular bedroom, with a bed much smaller than Nanny's.

We opened the closet and rummaged through some small boxes. Just a bunch of papers. Kathy had an idea: "Let's jump on the bed!" So leaving the closet door open, we stood on Pop-Pop's bed, held hands and jumped. As this wound down, I glanced into the closet and noticed a tall, black umbrella. I hopped off of the bed and grabbed it. "Let's open the umbrella and jump on the bed and pretend that we're singing in the rain, like that guy in the movie," I said.

I tried to open the umbrella but it pinched my fingers, so I handed it to Kathy. It pinched her fingers, too, but she got it open. And when she did, it began to rain dollar bills! They fell all over the bed and more were stuck in the spokes of the umbrella. At first, we were gleeful and thought that God must have sent us a miracle. Should we scoop up the money and give it to Dad next week? Put it back in the umbrella and never say a word? Tell Pop-Pop what we did and say we're sorry? Tell Nanny because she was the boss? Before we could make up our minds, we heard the key in the front door lock, and just stood there, frozen. It was Nanny.

"Young ladies, you were told not to go into . . . well, what have we here?" I detected a slight smile on her face, as she continued, "Where did you find this money? Located his hiding place, did you? Thank you for that."

I was confused, and even more so when she gave Kathy and me one dollar each and told us we could spend it or give it to our Dad. Then she said that we needed to go to bed early that night before Pop-Pop got home from his job at Campbell's Soup. She took the umbrella and the money and placed it on the dining room table.

Kathy and I were not tired, but we did as we were told. Once we got into bed, we decided to play a game that we called 'spit on backs'. One at a time, we pulled up our nightgowns, spit on our index finger and drew something, which the other person had to guess at. I preferred going last because it was relaxing and I liked going to sleep right after that. But just when it was my turn, we heard voices in the dining room. Nanny and Pop-Pop were arguing, so we called it quits, plugged our ears with our fingers, and fell asleep.

On the next Sunday, we all met for dinner where Mom and the baby were living. Since we did not want to get in trouble with Dad, we slipped the two dollars to Mom.

Dad made the announcement that our family would be back together soon. The application to McGuire Gardens had been approved, and to celebrate we were all going to my Aunt Dean's house in Williamstown, the night before we moved in. Dad and the two oldest boys were already living there, and my Aunt planned a feast for our family.

On the big night, Aunt Dean served macaroni salad, hot dogs, hamburgers, potato chips, and soda – all of my favorites. Best of all, nobody bugged me about eating too much of this, or too little of that. After dinner, we played games with my older cousins, Sonny and Sharon.

During a game of jacks, Sharon commented, "Your Dad keeps calling the place McGuire Gardens like it's a mansion or something. But you do know, don't you, that youse are moving to the Projects."

Sharon was often not nice to me; she favored Kathy. Hearing the smug tone in her voice, and having no idea that there was any stigma attached to living in the Projects, I assumed that this was just more of her usual meanness and simply quipped, "Yeah, sure."

The next day, I got my initial impression of McGuire Gardens: huge and confusing. All the buildings looked exactly alike – two-story rectangular rows built of brick. And there seemed to be *hundreds* of them. I worried that if I walked even a short distance, I would never be able to find my way back home.

Aside from the house numbers, the only way to tell your house from anyone else's was by how the yard and flower beds looked. Some yards were well-kempt and tidy, others scorched and uncared for. Unfortunately, ours was of the latter variety. The rental office provided free grass seed, stakes, twine, and bags of soil; hoses and push mowers were available to check out for a day. Taking advantage of all that, I did my best to spiff up the yard, but to no avail. All I knew to do was to sprinkle the yard with grass seed, then water it. Nothing ever grew, and I could always tell my house by the barren yard.

One year I hoped to earn some money by selling flower seeds. I saw an ad in a magazine – just for filling out an order form, the company would send me a box of flower seeds to sell. The price was five cents a pack, and I could keep a penny. They did not sell very well, but I did earn enough to buy a few packs of Four O'Clocks for myself. I planted them with care, and they grew to be tall and stately. They even produced their own seeds, which I collected, so that I could replant them the next spring. I was quite proud of my garden. It was the only spot of color during the summer amongst our otherwise brown lawn and unattended flowerbeds.

Life in the projects was very much indexed by the seasons, and of course, I liked summer the best, when the neighborhood came alive with scores of children playing outside. Jump rope, hopscotch, jacks, and tag were my favorite daytime activities. Despite the heat and humidity, and the mosquitoes at night, a favorite pastime was also catching lightning bugs. I would snip off their lighted tails with my fingernail and adorn my wrist with that part of their dead bodies. I pretended that I was wearing a diamond bracelet, and surprisingly, the light shone for several minutes. But I ceased this torturous practice when a neighborhood girl told me that I would serve time in Purgatory for it.

The neighborhood garbage was gross in the summer, yet I found a way to make it a source of income. The collection site was at the curb near my house. I avoided that area on garbage days until the cans were emptied, but one day I had the idea of returning some of the empty cans to their owners. I'd knock on their doors to let them know. Houses that had fewer kids often gave me a few pennies for my trouble, and occasionally a nickel.

But then the whole host of neighbors' kids caught on to my scheme and a local kid mafia developed. Linda Gayle, the neighborhood bully, declared that *she herself* would return the nickel cans; the rest of us had to share the penny cans then give her half of what we collected. Chicken-livered me acquiesced. It would be years before I gained enough confidence to take on that puny, big-mouthed bully.

During the warmer months, vendors walked through the neighborhood selling their wares. There were three that I particularly remember by the unique way they announced their approach; one sold apple taffies, the other tomatoes, and the last clothes props. They chanted loudly about these goods for sale with a lyrical rhythm that you almost could have jumped rope to.

Winter was an entirely different story. It snowed frequently and heavily, and few people ventured out of their homes unless it was necessary. The winds were so strong that snowdrifts blocked our front door, and we had to use the back door exclusively. No buses ran to St. Joseph's in any season, so we kids walked miles in the snow – literally. When we returned home from school, we all pulled off our mittens and put them on the radiator. The resulting melt water made the heater sizzle and steam. Our hands were often too cold to unzip our jackets, so Mama had to help.

ANN MARIE, KATHY, Tommy, EDDIE, Jimmy + Rosem.

Dressed for Easter Sunday in front of our apartment in the Projects, Camden, New Jersey.

If my father were alive today, he would be hard-pressed to list every job he had during our time in the Projects. I remember a few which were my favorites. For instance, one summer he drove the Jolly Roger ice cream truck. Kathy and I often rode with him, and he taught us how to make banana splits and sundaes. More importantly, we could indulge in any treat on the truck. He always made it a point to stop by our neighborhood, where the rest of my siblings also got to order anything they wanted.

For about a year, Dad worked as a baker and came home from work with white bags full of cream puffs, jelly donuts, cinnamon rolls, and cookies. All of us kids huddled by the window around 6 PM every work night, waiting to catch a glimpse of him walking down the street. Suddenly one of us would shout, "Here he is, here he is!" and minutes later we would get to gorge ourselves on sugary pastry.

Dad also worked for the Extermination Corporation. The company provided him with a car and materials, and he sprayed people's houses for bugs, by appointment. Sometimes he took one of us kids. We liked it because his route always included a stop at a tap room (never the one Nanny had taken us to), where we got to enjoy orange soda and pretzels, or red and white pistachios from a machine. I noticed that most people paid him in cash, and I wondered if he used some of that money for those stops. Maybe that is why he didn't work there very long.

Between jobs, we were on welfare. The state of New Jersey paid our rent and gave us a food voucher, but many other bills went unpaid. Mom had no money to go to the laundromat, and dirty clothes covered the floor of the pantry because the hamper was full. She washed diapers in the bathtub and put them on the radiators to dry during the winter. They were stiff as boards when they went on the babies' bottoms (and at one point, out of seven kids, she had three babies in diapers: Jimmy, Rosemary, and Billy).

The pantry was also the place where we stored our food. Sometimes mice gnawed into the cereal boxes. If I saw a hole in a box,

I was sure to proceed very carefully, and thankfully never poured a mouse into my bowl.

The food voucher consisted of a series of short white papers. At the checkout stand, each and every item purchased had to be hand-written on that form, and then added up by the checker – it took forever. I was the one who went shopping with Mom and saw how shoppers behind us left the line as soon as she pulled out those papers. Sometimes she sent me to the Acme by myself with those darn welfare forms. I hated using them, and not just because of the way that the checkers would roll their eyes or the length of time it took, but also because I felt ashamed and low-class to purchase groceries in such a way. As soon as Kathy was old enough, I would force her to go with me – and then make a hasty exit once we got to the check stand.

Just across the street stood a neighborhood of residential homes, which, unlike ours, didn't all look the same. Those facing the Projects were often barricaded by cyclone fencing. Those folks across the street had more money than we did, so I was always sure to trick-or-treat there. Residents in the Projects usually gave you a lollipop or a piece of bubble gum. The neighbors across the street often gave a full-sized candy bar!

The projects were my home for six years – the longest period of my childhood spent in any single place. Though I did not know it at the time, families could not be evicted from the projects for failing to pay their rent, which made the neighborhood a sort of last stand for folks in dire financial straits. But a family *could* be evicted for not meeting the low-income requirements, and as things turned out, that's exactly what eventually happened to us . . . though not before I would learn plenty of lessons at the parochial school I attended, Saint Joseph's Catholic.

Chapter 2:

THE LIE THAT WORKED

I stood in the kitchen, in my slip, waiting for Mom to finish ironing our uniform blouses. She did Kathy's first, and I sighed, wondering why I always had to be last. I knew better than to actually ask, as I'd already heard Mom's reasoning dozens of times: *Because you are the oldest.* It seemed to me that being the oldest should afford certain privileges, not punishments, and yet there were many times when I resented my status . . . for instance, at Easter if one of the chocolate bunnies had a big chip missing from its ear, the defective treat would be given to me.

Finally, Mom handed Kathy's blouse to her and picked up the sprinkler bottle to wet mine.

"Please Mom, no sprinkling. It makes my blouse feel damp and uncomfortable."

"Sorry, honey. I need to get these wrinkles out," she replied.

"Okay, I guess. I do like it when my blouse is clean." But I noticed that it didn't look very white anymore. In fact, it was almost grey. Since it was the last day of school, I didn't really think that I needed a clean blouse. But then again, it was report day, and that was a big deal at St. Joseph's.

I ran upstairs to finish dressing. Next came the hunter-green jumper. I had outgrown the one from St. Joseph's; this one was from Woolworth's. The material was flimsy, and I had to sew on the diamond-shaped "SJS" patch myself. I'd tried so many times to get it straight, but still, it was crooked, and now there were holes around the patch where I'd ripped it off to start over. It was also too small, and I wondered if Kathy was going to have to wear it next year or if we would get new uniforms. The thought was fleeting because I knew that either way, this ugly uniform would not see use for at least three months.

Walking to school that morning, I remembered what Sister Lucita had told my third-grade class the previous day. She'd said that Father Casey would be the priest distributing pupils' report cards. I liked Fr. Casey. He always smiled and said "hello" to me. He and my mother had attended Camden Catholic High School together, so it felt as though I had a special connection to him. Plus, he was really nice-looking. I also just knew in my heart that I had earned good grades and Fr. Casey might praise my good work, once he had a look at my report card.

I thought about Sister's instructions: "Even if you already have your report card, your eyes will be on Father Casey. You will pay attention, and you will be courteous as he shares his commentary about your fellow classmates. Do not think that I am not aware that it will be the last day of school. If you disobey me, your teacher next year will know about it, and she will keep her eye on you."

After lunch, Fr. Casey finally walked into the classroom. It was very hot, and even for Camden, New Jersey, in June, exceptionally humid. Though the windows were wide open, I was sweating. Despite that, all of us students sat rigidly still, hands neatly folded on our desks, maintaining the decorum that Sr. Lucita expected.

I sat quietly with my classmates, my heart pounding as Fr. Casey started calling pupils in order of their last name. After what seemed like forever, he reached L. Next was M, as in McCusker.

"Molly Malone," Fr. Casey called. Molly walked slowly up to Fr. Casey, but I did not hear one word that he said – my head was spinning because I was next! I had thought about covering up my sloppy "SJS" patch and had practiced that over lunch recess – but I ended up deciding that that looked stupid as if I was getting ready to say the

Pledge of Allegiance. So I readied myself to stand and walk to the front of the class, maintaining my best posture.

"Erin O'Malley," Fr. Casey called.

Oh no – he skipped me! Not daring to move my head, I tried to make eye contact with Sr. Lucita, but she was looking at Fr. Casey, just like she had told us to do. All kinds of possible reasons for the mistake swirled through my head, but I told myself to be patient and 'offer it up,' as we had often been told, remembering that God rewards sacrifice.

Fr. Casey called out forty-three names that day, but the forty-fourth – mine – was never called.

Fr. Casey gave us all a blessing for a joyous summer, told us to obey our parents, and say our prayers. Then he kindly dismissed the class.

Row by row, my classmates quietly left the room, as did Fr. Casey. As he neared the door, he quickly glanced at me, and I thought that I saw sadness on his face. Surely he was aware that he had not called my name? Didn't he see me still sitting in my seat even after my row left the classroom?

With no idea what else to do, I remained in my seat and waited for Sr. Lucita to notice me. Only when the classroom had emptied did she turned toward me.

"Yes, Miss McCusker?"

"Sister, I didn't get my report card."

Instead of shuffling through her desk, finding it, and turning it over to me, she made the comment, "I am aware of that, Miss McCusker." There was a pause, and she began to erase the chalkboard, her back to me.

She continued in an icy voice. "And are you aware that your parents have not paid one penny of tuition since you have been at this school? Not for any of you McCusker children. And I understand that there are more of you to come. This is not a free school. How do you think you are provided this education? Until your tuition is paid, you will not receive your report card."

I felt my face flush and tried not to cry, but my eyes filled with tears. I had no idea that my parents had never paid tuition – I might not have even known that there *was* a tuition! The sense of shame was overpowering. I wanted to bolt out the door. Instead, I said, "Yes, Sister. May I please be excused?"

Sr. Lucita did not answer right away. Instead, she walked to her desk and withdrew my report card.

"Ann Marie? You may have a quick look."

Then she placed the card onto her desk and went back to erase the board, adding that I had done very well in third grade.

I went to her desk and took a peek, feeling a flush of pride and relief as I saw my grades. "Thank you, Sister. May I please be excused?"

"You may," she said, in a voice that had regained a little warmth. "And just so you know, this was not my decision."

Walking home, I picked at that stupid crooked patch. Then without thinking about it, I tucked my fingers under the poorly sewn emblem and ripped it off, tearing an even bigger hole in the fabric. I was tempted to toss the emblem into the gutter, but thought better of the impulse and put it in my pocket instead.

Ginny Boothroyd, who lived at the other end of my building, was a few feet behind me and saw what I did. She had a trim, neatly fitting uniform, even though she also lived in the projects.

"You're going to get in trouble, Ann Marie!"

"I don't care, Ginny."

"Well, I'm going to be in trouble, too, once my Mom and dad see my report card. I didn't do so good. How were your grades?"

Ginny was a year younger than me, so I felt no need to impress her.

"Didn't get my report card, cuz my family didn't pay tuition. Hey! Youse guys don't have much money either. How come you got your report card?"

In a proud voice, Ginny said, "Monsignor excused us."

"Well, how did that happen?"

"Don't know, but we got free uniforms, too. And two new uniform blouses at Christmas when they give stuff to the poor."

Why had this kind of assistance not been extended to my family? It didn't seem right. We were better Catholics than the Boothroyds. I was raging inside at the unfairness of it all by the time Ginny said, "Wanna stop at that bank on the way home? Sometimes the lady in the glass cage puts a lollypop in a drawer, that pops out to give it to you."

"Okay, I guess."

When I arrived home, Kathy had already changed into play clothes and was outside. I asked her if she had gotten her report card.

"Nope. Sister said we have to pay money to get it. Did you get yours?"

"No," I responded. "So did you tell Mom?"

"No, I forgot."

Deciding to take my sister's lead, I also said nothing, and neither one of my parents asked. We were so used to having no money, being hounded by bill collectors, and worrying about having enough food to eat, that none of us could spare much concern about the coming year at St. Joseph's. So the summer passed with all of the usual trappings of our lives, including a new baby. Then it was time to return to school.

For fourth grade, I had Sister Violet. She was not known for being as strict as Sr. Lucita; in fact, she had a reputation for being more kind. But just in case, her forty-six students were all perfect angels on that first day. Less than an hour before dismissal, a messenger entered the classroom and gave a note to Sr. Violet. After reading it, she looked up straight at me.

"Miss McCusker, Mother Superior would like to see you immediately, in her office."

My mind raced as I climbed the ancient stairway to her office. I had never even been on the second floor of the building. You had to be in at least sixth grade to go up there, and doing so on my own was intimidating. It added to my worries that I had no idea where Mother Superior's office was.

I passed a large statue of Baby Jesus and Mother Mary and quickly asked for a blessing. It must have worked because I found the office moments later. Surely I couldn't be in any trouble? To my recollection, Mother Superior and I had never exchanged one single word. Nonetheless, she had loomed as a frightening presence on the edges of my school-day world.

Mother Superior walked out of her office and smiled at me, even as her secretary was saying, "Miss McCusker is here to see you." But did I imagine that her smile quickly became a frown? I looked at the floor and waited for her to speak.

"Come into my office please and take a seat."

"Yes, Mother."

Mother Superior was right behind me. After entering the room, she walked to a file cabinet, removed a file and took her seat behind a huge desk. "Look up at me, please." I did.

She rifled through the file and held some papers in her hand. "I know that your family does not have a phone, but do you have mail?"

"Excuse me, Mother?"

"I asked if your family gets mail delivered by the postal service, Miss McCusker?"

"Yes, Mother."

"Then how is it that I have in my hand, a half dozen copies of letters requesting that one of your parents contact me regarding your unpaid tuition bill? Are you aware that your family has not paid a penny's worth of tuition for you, your sister, or your brother? Do you suppose that your family believes that attending St. Joseph's is free, like the public schools?"

"I don't know, Mother."

"Well now *you* know, don't you? So I am entrusting you to personally deliver this letter to your parents when you get home. Let them know that I will be calling you in to see me tomorrow, expecting an answer to this letter. Is that clear?"

"Yes, Mother."

"You may be excused."

Walking home I was filled with dread. I knew there was no chance that my parents could pay any tuition, so I thought about ways that I could make some money. I had sold those flower seeds from the mail order company last year and made over four dollars. Would an amount like that be enough to help?

What if that letter was kicking us out of Catholic school? What if I had to go to school with Protestants! I could never stay in God's grace if I went to school with Protestants. Also, Dad told us that their schools were way behind the Catholic schools in terms of quality.

On the other hand, if I went to a Protestant school, I would not have to wear a stupid uniform. I could wear regular clothes! Only after a moment's reverie did I remember that I had very little in the way of regular clothes. And so the worries continued until I arrived home.

"Mom! Where are you? Mom?"

"Ann Marie, hush up your voice! Both the babies are asleep!"

She came into the kitchen, opened the refrigerator, and took out a package of hamburger. She often let me take a "pinch full" after she opened the large package, which I would salt and pop into my mouth, raw. But today I didn't want any. At that moment I was so preoccupied by my meeting with Mother Superior and the letter I held in my hand, that food held none of its usual interest for me.

Mom's gait was slow and deliberate. She was pregnant with baby number seven. In all of my early childhood memories, I only remember my mother wearing maternity clothes.

"Mom, Mother Superior called me upstairs to her office today, and asked me if we got mail, and then gave me this letter to give to you, and she wants you to answer it right away because she is going to call me into her office tomorrow. And I am *not* going to school tomorrow if you don't."

I went on to detail the whole story, then waited for her response, as she took a handful of hamburger and made a patty. At that moment, the baby wailed.

"Please go and get Billy from his crib, Annie-girl."

When I returned holding Billy, Mom had already put a saucepan on the stove to heat water for warming the baby's bottle. Bill was crying, and it was difficult to resume our conversation. I bounced him on my knee and talked to him, but he just arched his little back and looked over at Mom.

In a loud voice, my mother said, "I think that we need to have your father go and speak to Mother Superior."

"No!" I yelled but realized that my mother might think I was hollering at her. More gently, but still above the baby's screams, I added, "No, please Mama. I was so worried last year . . . " I stopped talking, deciding to wait until that darn bottle got warm enough to quiet Bill, but also recalling what had happened the previous year when Dad had decided to step in.

*** *** ***

That year my dad had worked at a shoe store. One night our whole family took the bus there after it was closed, and his boss had gone. Dad had the older five of us try on shoes. New shoes! And to my delight, we got to pick out any pair we wanted!

The shoes I chose were black patent leather with a tiny buckle. Best of all, they had Queen Anne heels, almost a whole inch high. I couldn't wait to get to school the next day to show off those shoes, certain that even Sr. Lucita would notice.

The next day in school, at exactly 10:00, four of the sixth-grade pupils – two girls and two boys – arrived to escort our class to the restroom. These older students were called 'safetys'. I hoped to one day have the honor of serving their role, which was to ensure that we stood quietly in line until it was our turn to go into a stall. Then we were to wash our hands and wait to return to the classroom, meanwhile not fooling around in any way.

I don't know why I did it, but when it was my turn, I looked down at my new shoes, and felt so happy, that I walked to the stall on my heels. I laughed out loud, imagining how I must look like a penguin. But the safety told me to stop carrying on, which immediately subdued me.

When we returned to class, the female safety told Sister that I had misbehaved. I jumped to my own defense, which seemed to make Sister even angrier. She grabbed my arm and made me stand on top of her desk. Next, she grabbed the yardstick and gave me three stinging swats across the back of my bare legs. It really hurt and I began to howl.

When I got home, I changed out of my uniform into shorts and hid my wounds under knee socks. But when I came downstairs wearing knee socks in the heat, Dad was on to me. The more he looked at those socks, the more I could not look at him. Finally, he told me to pull down my socks, and when I did, he asked me what the heck happened. I told him, and he became enraged - not at me, but at Sister. I was glad that he could see how unfair she had been.

The next morning, I expected that Dad would catch the bus to the shoe store as usual, but he told us that he had quit because he needed a better-paying job. Then he said that he was going to walk to school with Kathy, Tom, and me, because he wanted to speak to Sr. Violet. I wasn't sure what reasons he might have for speaking with Sister, but we were thrilled to have Dad's congenial company for the walk to school.

Dad walked Kathy and Tom to their classrooms, and then we went to mine.

"What are you going to say to Sister, Dad?"

"That I will rip her stockings off and beat *her* across her bare legs if she ever touches you again!"

"But Dad . . ." I began, but at that moment, in the door we walked.

Dad and Sr. Violet had never met, but my father walked right up to her, told her who he was, turned me around and said, "I would like you to take a look at the welts, the black and blue marks, on my daughter's leg!"

Sister suggested that they step outside the classroom and my father agreed. I took my seat, as did the rest of the pupils. I looked around and gave my classmates a nervous smile.

I could hear Dad hollering in the corridor, and I strained to hear Sr. Violet's words. Then she walked back into the classroom and told us to stand for the Pledge of Allegiance, which was followed by our morning prayers. Sister Violet never said a word to me about it, nor did she touch me again for the remainder of the year. Not that she would have had any cause – I was a well-behaved pupil, and even more so after her beating.

*** *** ***

Mom tested the milk's temperature by squirting some on her wrist and handed me the bottle. My mind returned to the present once Billy was eagerly sucking down his dinner, content enough to allow my conversation with Mom to continue, though at first, all three of us were quiet for a while.

I could not imagine what purpose it could serve to have Dad go to school with me this time around. While I was proud of him for sticking up for me the previous year, what could he possibly do this time? There was no money, and I knew it.

Dealing with invasive bill collectors had become part of our family routine. Whenever one knocked on the door, Mom would hide and have one of us kids answer, and tell the guy, "Our Mom is not at home." Expecting my parents to make even a small payment on that tuition bill would have been "Asking for the Man in the Moon" (a phrase that my mother used when one of us asked for something financially impossible). Only the previous day, Mom had sent me next door to borrow a dollar from our neighbor, so she could buy bread for lunches on our first day of school. I so hated doing that.

"When do you think we can pay St. Joseph's some money, Mom?" I finally asked.

"I have no idea, honey. But give me the baby and go get that letter out of your school bag." She rinsed off her hands, put Billy over her shoulder, and burped him.

"Oh! Be right back, Annie-girl. He needs his diaper changed."

I went to my room, pulled the letter out of my bag, and looked at it. What if she gave it to Dad and he did decide to go to school with me the next day? I was afraid of more conflict and already knew that there was no money to solve this problem.

Kathy walked into our bedroom and asked if I wanted to go outside and play.

"In a minute," I said.

"Wait for you outside." I walked back into the kitchen empty-handed. I had no plan at that point, other than perhaps buying some time, and hoping that this mess would all go away.

"I left the letter at school, Mom. I'll bring it home tomorrow."

"Okay, honey. I'll look at it tomorrow."

It was only September. I could not pretend to be sick for the rest of the year. So I went to school the next day.

All day I watched the clock, revising my story to Mother Superior every half hour or so. At one point my latest idea was to tell her that, "I was in the kitchen feeding the baby while Mom made hamburgers. Mom took the baby so's I could go get the letter, and as I handed it to her, Billy threw up all over it. It was so disgusting that she had to throw it away, and wonders if you could send another one home in a few weeks after Mom gets back from visiting her mother who lives in Virginia."

It was 2:30, only fifty more minutes to go when a messenger walked into the classroom. I had probably jinxed myself by vowing to not look at the clock until the bell rang.

Once again, it was up the ancient stairs and into the office – where I found Kathy sitting in the waiting area.

"What are you doing here?" I whispered to my little sister.

"Don't know. I just got called in. Do you know if we did something wrong, Ann Marie?"

"We didn't do a darn thing wrong. Let me do the talking, Kathy."

·   I half-expected to see Tommy, my second-grade brother, show up, too. Maybe her torture plan was to have him called in tomorrow. Then Eddie, my first-grade brother, the next day? I got so angry thinking about it. I wanted to scream at Mother to leave my brothers and sisters alone! But then Mother Superior called us into her office, and my bravado melted like a Popsicle in July.

"Hello, girls. I expect that you have some news for me. However, I see that your hands are empty. Does this mean that your parents ignored my request for a written response?"

Kathy looked at her hands and then focused her big blue eyes on me. I took one of her hands, and blurted out, "My Mother told me to tell you that Monsignor excused us."

This was entirely unrehearsed. It just fell out of my mouth. And immediately, the internal backlash began: *This is not a little white lie, not a venal sin. This is a big gigantic lie, a mortal sin! I need to take it back immediately.*

"Why didn't you . . . when did . . . why was I not informed?"

Mother Superior flushed. She picked up a file on her desk, looked up at us and said, "I am sorry, young ladies. Apparently, there has been a lack of communication. May I offer you each a piece of candy before you return to your classrooms?"

I had noted my sister eyeing that candy dish, and I had seen it the previous day. But, of course, we dared not indulge until invited.

On the way down the stairs, as Kathy busily unwrapped her butterscotch, I grabbed her. "Swear to God, Kathy. Not a word to Mom or Dad, okay? If you don't tell, you can play with my Tiny Tears doll any time without asking me. Okay?"

"Okay."

Kathy seemed content to be out of that office, enjoying her candy. I was not so happy. I knew that I was in big trouble and did not know what to do about it.

We went back to our classrooms and waited for the bell to ring. When it did, pupils filed to the coat closet to pick up coats and school bags. Since it was late September, most of us carried our coats home. I met Kathy at our designated spot, and together we walked over to the first-and-second-grade play yard to pick up Tommy and Eddie.

On the long walk home from school, I interacted very little with my siblings, other than to take their hands as we crossed the streets. I played and replayed a host of scenarios in my mind about how to fix what I had done. Telling my parents was not an option. I had to figure this out for myself.

Confessions were heard at St. Joseph's every noon hour while the pupils were at recess. We were strongly encouraged to go at least once a week in order to remain in God's grace. I would be going tomorrow and hoped that Fr. Casey would be hearing confession. But what if it was the Monsignor?

Monsignor!! If he was not hearing confession, he would be in the rectory.

During noon recess, the rectory was open to pupils. For the most part, we would only go there to have something blessed. Good Catholic children never used a new rosary, or wore a holy medal or scapular, without having it blessed by a priest.

It was a very long night. I was terrified that if I died in my sleep, I would go straight to Hell. Clearly, I needed to stay awake all night. That was not so hard as long as my parents were awake. I crept halfway down the stairs and just listened to their conversation, occasionally peering over the banister, then quickly ducking down. Dad was drinking his beer and smoking, and Mom was eating a Hershey bar (she kept a stash of sweets hidden from us kids).

Billy started to cry, so Dad went to their downstairs bedroom to pick him up, while Mom warmed up his bottle. Then Dad went to bed, and Mom stayed up to feed the baby. Finally, Mom went to bed, and I was left alone with my thoughts and fears. Now, what should I do? I decided to get out of my pajamas and put on my uniform. I would lie quietly on the top of my covers and wait for morning.

I must have fallen asleep because when I awoke, Mom was looking over at me on my top bunk, saying, "And what are you doing in bed already dressed?"

"I, uh, well, I woke up early and could not go back to sleep so I just thought I should get ready for school, Mama."

"Oh, all right. What kind of sandwich do you want in your lunch today?"

"Baloney, cheese, and lettuce, please."

"You're not sick, are you?"

When in trouble, I was the kind of kid who just wanted to get it over with. It was sheer torture to me whenever I did something wrong, and Mom would say, "Just wait until your father gets home!" So I decided not to opt for the sick card, and get myself to school. My only hope . . . dream . . . fervent prayer . . . was to make it until noon recess without being called to Mother Superior's office.

11:59. I made it! "No running in the corridors," shouted one of the safetys from some place I could not see. I walked as fast as I could, went into the church, made the Sign of the Cross with the Holy water, genuflected before a pew, and looked toward the confessionals. One of my classmates came to my row to say her penance, and in a quiet voice I asked, "Who's hearing confessions today?"

Ever so solemnly, Lorraine held up her hand for silence. She was saying her penance and not to be interrupted. I hoped that her sin list was short. Her eyes were closed, her hands folded in prayer. I tried to be respectful, but finally, I'd had enough.

"Look, Lorraine, just quickly tell me which priest you spoke to! Please!"

"Okay, okay," she whispered. But for some reason, her voice became embarrassingly loud when she added, "It's Fr. Casey, Ann Marie!"

I genuflected at the end of the pew, walked briskly out the door, and blessed myself with Holy water. Then I headed for the rectory.

I rang the rectory doorbell, and after a short wait, the housekeeper answered. She was broad, with white hair pulled back into a bun, and wore black tie shoes with wide heels. Her shoes reminded me of the ones that my great-grandmother always wore. Her white apron had dark smudges on it, and she smelled delicious. I was suddenly aware of being hungry, having left my lunch sack in the cloakroom.

"Good afternoon, Mrs. LoPresti, may I please speak with the Monsignor?"

"Monsignor is having his lunch, child. Have you an item that you want to be blessed?"

"No, ma'am. It's personal."

"If you have a confession to make, Fr. Casey is hearing them in the church."

"No, ma'am. Well, sort of in a way. But it is really important that I speak to Monsignor before I go back to class."

"What is your name, child?"

I told her and she gestured to the vestibule of the house. I walked in and sat myself on a very pretty chair. I liked this room and wished we had such a nice room in our house. Then my thoughts shifted to the matter at hand - what would I say to Monsignor? I began to rock back and forth in the pretty chair. *I will tell him about the lie.*

I had never been alone with Monsignor in my life. He said the High Mass and had a very nice singing voice. But I could not remember if he had one of those big rings that I was supposed to kiss, like the Bishop. I was fretting about this important detail when he walked into the room.

I stood up, as we were told to do any time an adult enters the room. I looked at his hand but could neither confirm nor refute the ring, because he was holding his napkin from lunch. So I just stood there like a dummy, not saying a word.

"Please be seated, Miss McCusker. Mrs. LoPresti gave me the impression that we have urgent business to discuss. Is that correct? So let's begin, shall we?"

His eyes were kind and attentive, and I found his invitation so sincere that I began to pour out my painful story. And then I saw the big red ring on his finger.

Not seeming to realize why I had suddenly paused, Monsignor encouraged me to continue. I got to the part about the Boothroyd family being excused from paying tuition. Then my own family's dire financial situation and how I could not bring myself to tell my parents about the tuition issue. And finally, I wrapped up the whole drama with my lie to Mother Superior.

I leaned back slightly in my pretty chair and sighed, but then quickly sat straight up, and awaited my judgment.

"Ann Marie, let me say that I do indeed excuse your parents from tuition. Had your family only come to me, we could have taken care of this some time ago. Please tell them what I have said, and that I or Fr. Casey will be stopping by some evening soon to get to know all of you better. Having said that, we still face the issue of your lying to Mother Superior, do we not?"

"Yes, Father, I mean, Monsignor. I will go to Confession."

"You just have."

He stood, and so did I. Monsignor raised his right hand and made the sign of the cross, saying, "*In Nomine Patris, et Filii, et Spiritus sanctum. Amen.*"

"*Amen.*" I bent down on one knee and kissed his ring.

*** *** ***

Reflecting back upon this pivotal time with the benefit of hindsight, I understand how formative it was for me. I learned that I could fix things by myself. I learned that I could take an active role, and not succumb to being victimized. And I learned to lie when it was a question of survival.

In front of Saint Joseph's Catholic School before receiving my first Holy Communion, 1958.

Chapter 3:

MISS COURICO

It did not take very long for me to realize that I was one of the luckiest fifth graders at St. Joseph's Catholic School. Out of twenty-seven teachers, twenty-five were Franciscan nuns. The other two were 'lay teachers' and I had been assigned to one of them.

I knew right away that this year was going to be different. The very first thing that I noticed about Miss Courico was that she wore regular clothes: a skirt, stockings with seams, and high-heeled shoes. Her hands, unencumbered by the folds of a habit, she used freely in sweeping movements, adding emphasis to her words. She also wore a charm bracelet on each wrist – a novelty for us kids, so accustomed to nuns who eschewed jewelry, unless you counted the big-beaded rosaries wrapped around their waists.

Miss Courico was young and pretty, with a great big smile. She greeted us on that first day as though she was actually happy to be our teacher, clasping her hands together as she said, "I am *so* delighted to meet my new pupils."

We stood for prayer and the Pledge of Allegiance, before resuming our seats. Then, without prompt, we opened our desks and removed our religion books – but Miss Courico said, "No, no, we are not doing that yet. I would like to teach you a new song. How does that sound?"

I searched my memory to see if it was a Holy day or a feast day that I had forgotten, as Miss Courico directed our attention to the chalkboard at the back of the room. Written there in her careful cursive were the lyrics to a song called 'Freddie and his Fiddle.' I couldn't remember ever having been taught a secular song at St.

Joseph's, although as things turned out, 'Freddie' was only the first of many songs we would learn that year which had absolutely nothing to do with Jesus or the Virgin Mary.

"You follow along and read the lyrics, while I sing the melody, students."

Out of her mouth emerged the most beautiful singing voice I had ever heard. Her charm bracelets jingled, making their own music as she led us in song. Her enthusiasm proved contagious, and we all sang along with abandon. As for me, I was in love.

After a wonderful first few days of class, a potential discipline problem arose. Dale, a fellow pupil, was unable to recite a prayer. Moments like these were frightening for most of us, in part, because we never knew if the punishment would target the offender, or be extended to the entire class. There had been numerous times in years past when one of the Sisters had decided that an entire class was to blame. We would then be made to line up and endure swats from a paddle as we passed by the angry nun.

I had shared the same nun with Dale a couple of times in earlier grades, and I always felt sorry for him. He, like some of my other classmates, struggled to learn the Mass in Latin. This feat was required by the school. By sixth grade, we had to recite, and later sing, the High Mass in its original language.

Miss Courico would go around the room, each pupil reciting several lines from a particular part of the Mass. On this day, we were working on the *Credo*, which was especially long and difficult: "*Credo in Unum Deum, Patrem omnipotent, Factorem Caeli et Terrae* . . ."

When it was Dale's turn, he said nothing at all.

Here we go! I looked up at the ceiling, noting for the hundredth time that many of the overhead lights had burned out. The silence was heavy with foreboding. Not one of us dared look directly at Dale or Miss Courico. But I heard the click of her high-heeled shoes as she walked toward Dale's first-row desk. When she stopped directly in front of him, I finally ventured a look in that direction.

"Dale, is there any part of the Mass that you know by heart?"

"Yes, ma'am."

"And what part is that, Dale?"

"I know the *Kyrie*, Miss Courico," he responded sheepishly.

Chuckles broke out around the classroom. The *Kyrie* was a whopping two lines long, each line repeated multiple times.

"Silence!" said Miss Courico to the class. Then she went on, "Can you please recite the *Kyrie* for the class, Dale?"

"*Kyrie eleison, kyrie eleison, kyrie eleison. Christe elesion, christe elesion, christe elesion. Kyrie elesion, kyrie eleison, kyrie eleison.*"

"Excellent, Dale. Keep up the good work."

With Miss Courico as my teacher, I actually looked forward to my time in the classroom. I didn't have to worry about those rigid nuns, who seemed to enjoy punishing their students, and were short on praise of any kind.

In fifth grade, my imagination about romance began to bloom, and I convinced myself that Miss Courico had a crush on Fr. Casey. I had learned from my mother that Fr. Casey's first name was Jack, and I had heard the only other lay teacher call Miss Courico Janet. *Can you imagine – they have the same initials! Jack Casey and Janet Courico!* I scribbled "JC + JC" in my notebook, realizing with awe that not only were their initials the same, they shared initials with Jesus Christ! Adding a cross to the top of my page, and writing yet another JC, I fantasized about how happy my teacher would be when she walked into her classroom one day to see Fr. Casey waiting for her! Unfortunately, things did not quite play out in the way I had imagined.

One cold December morning, I walked into the classroom barely able to unbutton my coat. My fingers were so cold, they refused to move.   Only with careful resolve did I manage to make my fingers work, take off my coat, and hang it on my assigned hook.

Only then did it fully register with me that Fr. Casey was there, and there was no sign of Miss Courico.

"Please take your seats, students," said Fr. Casey. "I have some news to tell you."

He went on to explain that our beloved teacher had burned her eyes the day before, as she changed one of those long, thin lights that hung from the ceiling. She had been advised to wait for the janitor, who came to the school every Thursday but had decided to do it herself.

"At the present time, her eyes are weepy and swollen, and she must keep them bandaged for at least two weeks," Fr. Casey told us. "She will return when her doctor tells us that it is okay. Your substitute should be arriving soon. I encourage all of you to make your teacher proud by behaving yourselves, and by keeping Miss Courico in your daily prayers."

A dozen hands shot into the air: "Will she be back after two weeks?" "Can we write to her?" "Is she in pain?"

Sitting there, I recalled a moment from the previous day's math lesson. Her black sweater had been covered with chalk dust as she explained how to multiply and divide fractions. She had given us a pop quiz, then dismissed us for lunch. When we returned to the classroom, she sported a huge smile while passing out the corrected quiz. Finally, she walked to the front of the classroom.

"Students, I could not be more proud of each and every one of you. Fractions are difficult to master, and you have done very, very well. So let's put away the math, and sing a song. Who wants to pick one? Raise your hand!"

Remembering that moment, I opened the top of my desk and pulled out my quiz. My score was 100%, and Miss Courico had written, "Excellent work, Ann Marie." I returned that cherished quiz back to my desk at the exact moment that our substitute walked into the classroom. It was Mother Superior. My heart sank.

The classroom felt dark without Miss Courico, even though the snow seemed to make everything outside look brighter.

I soon lost my enthusiasm for school. It had not taken me long to learn to hunger for the praise that Miss Courico doled out with kindness, but Mother Superior's style was just the opposite. She taught by shaming us. God help us if she ever got around to the Latin of High Mass. I could not imagine what she would do with the likes of poor Dale.

Worried that Miss Courico might never be coming back to us, I stepped up my prayers for her. Meanwhile, Mother Superior was made cross by our constant inquiries about when Miss Courico might return, so we gave up asking. It never occurred to me that these questions could have hurt her feelings. To me, she seemed heartless.

School recessed for a week over Christmas, and during that time, I managed to convince myself that Miss Courico would be back after the holidays. So on the morning of January 3, 1961, I dressed for class with anticipation. I even walked to school with Linda Gayle, who I normally avoided. She was in my class, and lived with her grandparents in the Projects, in the building across from ours. Even though Linda was short and skinny, she was a big-mouthed bully who always wanted to fight. One wrong word and she would bellow, "Choose you out!" They were colloquial words in that place and time for challenging someone to a fistfight. A few years before, to my personal humiliation, I had allowed her to commandeer my garbage can collection project.

I felt puzzled about why Linda had made such an effort to catch up with me on this particular day, and we said little during our walk. It embarrasses me to this day to admit that I was afraid of her. But on this particular day, I felt so happy that I knew that I could not possibly say anything to incur her wrath. Boy was I wrong!

We walked into our classroom together that morning. There was no sign of Mother Superior, but also no Miss Courico. Just as the bell rang, an eighth-grader walked into the classroom and told us that Fr. Casey would be starting up class that day – and darned if I did not start to cry. Linda Gayle was all over it. The moment the eighth grader left, Linda shouted, "What a BABY!!! Little baby Ann Marie misses her teacher so much that she is crying like a baby! Can anyone find this baby a bottle so she will shut up!"

"You shut up yourself, Linda Gayle." My voice was weak and tentative. I had watched her beat the heck outa girls twice her size, so I seriously considered telling her that *I take it back,* even as she hauled her skimpy body to my seat and began punching me, calling me a "chicken" and a "baby." In a moment of unprecedented courage, I started punching her back – and as it happened, I whipped her skinny butt.

Fr. Casey broke it up. Linda and I both stopped thrashing about once we realized who it was, though she ran from us toward the door. And wouldn't you know whose arms she ran right into? Yep – Miss Courico!

I wanted to be the one to run to Miss Courico! How could this possibly be? I just stood there. And I smiled at Miss Courico. At least it was Fr. Casey, and not she, who administered the punishment. Linda Gayle and I had to stay after school for a week and dust the statues in every classroom. But I did not care. Miss Courico, my refuge and sanctuary, was back.

My love of singing may have started at home with my dad, but Miss Courico refined this interest in me. She was the first of a handful of teachers who helped me see the world in a different way – and she did this not by singling me out to tell me how special I was. She made each and every one of her students believe that they possessed a special gift. She uncovered and nurtured us by finding that little bit of divinity in each pupil. I'll always be grateful for her presence in my life at such a critical time. She helped me feel intelligent, talented, and worthy.

In my eleven-year-old mind and heart, when it came to grown-ups whom I truly revered, Miss Courico was right up there with my father.

Chapter 4:

THAT ONE THANKSGIVING

My teacher for sixth grade was Sr. Elizabeth. Her quiet, almost clipped speech presented quite a contrast to my third and fourth grade Sisters, who had tended to be dramatic and loud. I missed the respite of my beloved Miss Courico, but if I had to have another nun, Sr. Elizabeth would do just fine.

She added a touch of class to our morning greeting. *"Bonjour, ma soeur,"* the class would chant. *"Bonjour, mes eleves,"* Sr. Elizabeth would respond. Anything to get away from conjugating Latin verbs, but French? That was *tres magnifique. I'd love to learn French,* I thought, *but maybe all we'll learn is how to pray in French.* We learned more than that, though, and to this day I can still bless myself, say grace, and recite some portions of the Mass in that lovely language.

I also learned that Sr. Elizabeth had a good heart.

One morning in early November, she announced that our class was going to take on a project "for the poor" by providing a Thanksgiving dinner for an unfortunate family. For the first week, we were encouraged to bring in canned goods, and other nonperishable food items. In the second week, our class hosted a cupcake sale – every student was asked to bring a dozen or two.

My family barely managed to feed ourselves. I'd never tasted a homemade cupcake or cookie in my life. Bringing cupcakes felt impossible to me under the circumstances, so I hoped to get into Sr. Elizabeth's good graces by volunteering to help sell the goodies. I was one of eight students chosen to do so.

On sale day, we sold cupcakes over the lunch hour as well as after school – five cents for the pretty ones, two-for-five for the less decorated. With great envy, I helped students with their purchases, my mouth watering, wanting nothing else but to taste *just one of* those treats.

Our class did well. Sr. Elizabeth announced that we'd raised enough money, and contributed enough food, for some destitute family to "have a feast." She asked us how many of us had wagons, and could bring them to the convent on the day before Thanksgiving to help transport the food to the poor family. Sister told us that she would select each student privately, adding that we would need to check with our parents for approval.

One of my brothers had received a Red Flyer wagon the year before, for Christmas. With great eagerness, I volunteered. I could do this!

At the end of the school day before Thanksgiving, assuming I had not been selected to help since I had heard nothing in response, I went with the other students to the cloakroom to fetch my jacket. To my surprise, Sr. Elizabeth called me aside and asked if I could bring my wagon to the convent immediately. I was thrilled! I just knew that God would store up extra blessings in heaven for me for walking all the way home, back to the convent, and then to some poor family's home in wintry weather.

I rushed home, running as much of the two miles as I could. Breathlessly, I hurried into the house and grabbed Tom's wagon.

Mom spotted me before I could be off again. "Hey, hey, hey," she said. "Why are you home so early, and where do you think you're going?"

Having previously told my mother about our little class project, I brought her up to speed quickly, adding, "Okay, Mom?" She smiled in response, and I saw pride in her eyes. Feeling like God's chosen one, off I went, back to St. Joseph's.

It had just begun to snow, and I worried whether I could make the walk to some poor family's home with a loaded wagon. *At least the wagon will be empty on the way home,* I thought, *and unless this house is far away, I'll be home for dinner.* Fortunately, the snow remained light, and it was an easy, though chilling, walk.

When I arrived at the convent, I rang the bell and waited for the gate to open. Sr. Elizabeth came out with three other nuns, carrying many bags, which they piled into my wagon. Wordlessly, Sr. Elizabeth secured the load, as I waited for directions to the lucky family's house.

But all Sister said to me was, "Happy Thanksgiving. Go home now." Then she put an envelope into my snow-moistened pocket, turned, and went back inside.

I stood there for a moment, stupefied. My confused thoughts went to the envelope, and I felt an irresistible urge to look inside. It contained a large amount of money – a five-dollar bill, some ones, and some change!

And only then did I realize . . . my family and I were the poor ones for whom this gift was intended.

Chapter 5:

THE CENTRAL, ESSENTIAL PERSON

My life during the years that I lived at home revolved around my father. Our survival as a family depended upon his capacity to be the breadwinner. Sometimes he did a poor job of this, and other times he succeeded. His temperament was equally inconsistent. In the early years, he was playful and loving. Later, he would become a man whom I feared.

But during the six years when we lived in the projects (1957 - 1963), we may have run out of milk and had to put water on our morning cereal, but we always had a father who was fun and devoted to his family. This was particularly true in the evenings, after dinner.

It was then that he became the master entertainer. With nine children, no television, and few toys, he managed to dream up activities that kept us amused until bedtime. Sometimes we all did the "Irish jig," which he taught us, and danced right along with us. To this day, I can hear him saying, "toe, heel, cross, kick," as he clapped a sprightly beat. Other times, he hooted out Indian calls, challenging us to "get our Indian out." His grandmother had been Kickapoo, and as the story goes, a princess (of course).

Often, he sang, and my Dad had a beautiful voice. We kids would all join in; without any formal musical training, he taught us how to harmonize. Over the Christmas season, the local newspaper, the *Courier Post*, included an insert each day with the lyrics to many popular Christmas carols. My mother saved multiple copies. Those of us who could read each held a copy; those who couldn't just picked up the melody and lyrics. While Mama never danced or hoofed with us, she did join in the singing. In fact, as a grand finale, she would often agree to sing *Ava Maria* in Latin. Mom's voice was sweet, tender, and quiet. It reminded me of how she sang our lullabies.

Dad was also a fine storyteller. Despite having little formal education, he was articulate and quite theatrical. My favorite stories were about his wonderful dog, Shep. We heard of endless adventures that he and his beloved dog had together in his youth. He even wrote a song about Shep, which he would sing in his fine tenor voice. It always brought me to tears because it's a story of love and friendship.

One day our family went to Williamstown to visit my Aunt Bernadine and her family. During a lull in the gathering, I asked my Dad to sing that song about his dog, old Shep. To my astonishment, Bernadine shot my Dad a look and said, "For God's sake, Tommy, when are you going to tell these kids the truth!"

Puzzled, I could only manage an uncertain, "Dad?"

My father's gaze remained on the floor, as my Aunt burst out with, "Your father never had a dog named Shep." Then she took a quick sip from her coffee and lit a cigarette. My father took a long drink from his beer and also lit a cigarette.

Though confused, I still had no doubt that my father would rebut her lie, and break into song. But he did not. My stare implored him to speak, but he wouldn't meet my gaze. Instead, he blew smoke down at the floor, and said to his sister in a small voice, "Every child needs stories to cultivate their imagination." But that explanation did not work for me, and from that moment forward, I was never able to look at my father the same way again.

Maybe he believed what he said about telling stories, and had never dreamed that learning the truth would leave me feeling so betrayed.

Maybe he wished that he *had* owned a dog named Shep, to comfort him during his times of fear, and the betrayals he had suffered.

Maybe he would have explained . . . had I thought to ask him, before he died.

Chapter 6:

A BRIGHT SPOT

Dad got a job as a new car salesman at Rohrer Chevrolet in Camden, New Jersey. He had held so many jobs in the past, yet there was something different about this one. He seemed so very happy with this job, bragging about how much money he was making, and how much the management liked him. After sales, he brought home small yellow pieces of paper that were his commission slips. Each slip listed the amount of money that he would be paid on his next check. It became a family ritual to watch him get a blank piece of paper, add up the amounts on the yellow slips, and learn how much money he would be bringing home.

Even more exciting for us kids, he got to drive a brand-new Chevrolet Impala that he called a "demo." It was pale blue and smelled new – at least until the odor of his cigarettes took over. Somehow, the whole family managed to squeeze into that car for rides on his days off. Folks in the Projects would watch us, some even gathering around as we loaded up the family; ours was the only brand-new car in the neighborhood.

Next, we got a brand-new television set. We watched programs such as *The Lawrence Welk Show*, anticipating our favorite Chevrolet commercial, with its catchy lyrics and music. "See the USA in your Chevrolet," Dinah Shore would sing. Dad sang along, and so did the rest of us, jumping from our seats and crowding around him. Mama would watch from across the room, smile, then start laughing out loud. I'd never seen her so happy. She even looked different in those days. Her face had grown soft and peaceful, like it did when she sang a lullaby to one of the babies. Her big eyes seemed wider and brighter, and she began to groom herself better.

I was amazed by all of the fancy things that began to roll into our house! Mama got a new washer. Then came linoleum for all floors, a pink floral pattern, which replaced the worn, dull green flooring. There were new bunk beds for us kids, new clothes, and even new kinds of food. We were used to having hamburger patties, boiled potatoes, and some kind of canned vegetable pretty much every day, varied only by fish sticks on Friday. We had rarely enjoyed pork chops or steak, but now we were eating those foods regularly, not to mention ice cream for later in the evening. Mom got to play bingo every week at St. Joseph's, and each of us kids got a weekly allowance. My dad was very generous when he had money; at such times he clearly enjoyed life and felt happy to provide luxuries for his family.

We even took a vacation to Lake Lenape, Mays Landing, New Jersey, staying in a big cabin there for six days. This was the first real trip my family ever made, and every one of us felt ramped up with excitement over it. I got to go horseback riding for the first time, and loved it!

There was, however, one slight shadow, which clouded the joy of that idyllic vacation.

Every night Dad would go out and leave all of us kids in the cabin with Mom. We all assumed that he was going to some nearby town to drink his beer at a tavern, since the small grocery store at Lake Lenape did not sell it. I could tell that Mom did not like this. She would ask him to please "come back in an hour," then become distant and agitated for the many hours that he was gone. He never returned until long after everyone had fallen asleep.

One night, when everyone else was bedded down for the evening, I heard Dad struggling to get the key in the door. Once he got inside, he had trouble walking, but appeared to be heading for the bathroom. I silently watched him, pretending to be asleep. He unzipped his pants, but then fell to the floor short of his goal, and just laid there. I was alarmed – what could be wrong with him? – and hopped out of the double bed that I shared with Kathy. Even though I was nearly twelve years old, I knew nothing about drunks passing out.

When I reached Dad, he was fast asleep. I saw his penis. I knew what it was because I was very practiced at changing the boys' diapers. Perhaps I stared too long because I began to feel sinful.

The next morning I awoke with a sense of guilt and shame, irrationally worrying that Dad may have seen me stare. But he was alert and eager to tell us his plan for the day. In his big voice, Dad announced, "Today is pool day, tribe. I need to teach youse how to swim!"

Mama was afraid of water and didn't want to get in the pool, but I couldn't wait! It annoyed me, though, that I had to take ten-month-old Trish in with me. As Dad tried to teach us all how to swim, I could not follow his moves, since I was in the shallow end holding Trish. Finally, I sat her on one of the top steps of the pool so that I could try the doggie paddle myself.

I was only gone for a second, but when I turned back around, she was off the step and into the water. I will never forget that moment. Trish calmly floated, face up, with her eyes open. She was not struggling in any way. In fact, she had a very peaceful look on her face – so peaceful, that I thought she must be dead.

Horrified, I scooped her up into my arms. Trish rubbed her eyes, looked straight into my mine, and smiled. No one else had seen any of this.

That moment, and its surreal mixture of fear and serenity, haunts me to this day. I'm sure that this is partly because of my negligence – such a contrast to the pronounced sense of responsibility that I have always felt toward my siblings. But more than that, I find the whole event eerie; Trish had been so complacent, so calm, and had not struggled in the least, though she could very easily have drowned.

53

When we returned home from Lake Lenape, my parents bought a huge above ground swimming pool, and our home became the place where all the neighborhood kids wanted to be. Nobody in the Projects had such a luxurious thing; much later in life, I realized that the pool, plus the new Chevy parked at the curb, must have aroused suspicion among the management.

Among the many evictions that would occur in my family's future, this would be the only time we were tossed out for making *too much* money. The Projects management made inquiries to Rohrer Chevrolet and learned that my father's income far exceeded the qualifying amounts to live in McGuire Gardens. We received a thirty-day notice.

Within three weeks, my family rented a house and moved to a nice neighborhood in Cherry Hill, New Jersey; it was July of 1963. How I loved that house! The comfortable, sprawling lawn with lovely landscaping, and quaint two-story house made for a sharp contrast to the dull uniformity of the Projects. The place had only three bedrooms, but they were large. A huge front porch became a play area, though we were instructed to keep a watchful eye on the little ones. The sole drawback was that the front yard lay scarcely fifty yards from a four-lane freeway, but the backyard seemed to go on endlessly!

A neighbor told us that an elderly couple had lived in this house and that the Missus had moved to live with one of her children when her husband died. Those previous owners had made much of the back acreage into a vineyard. The area was still full of grape vines, set back from an orchard, which surrounded three sides of the house. The vines and the trees had been unattended for quite some time and provided an endlessly versatile landscape for games like hide-and-seek. There were even a couple of little shacks hidden among the trees, one of which I claimed as my own life-sized dollhouse.

The house had a full basement, crammed with ancient wine making equipment. Big barrels with wooden spigots flanked one of the walls. It was a dark and scary place; we kids would never venture down there alone.

The former residents had also left behind a large dining room table, a hutch with some china, and an Oriental rug. These accouterments made the dining room my favorite. Being in there made me feel like we were high-classed people. We only actually ate there when we had guests, which was almost never.

The first time we did have a guest in that house, Dad brought a younger woman home with him and told us that she was his long-lost cousin, Ronnie. He made a point of announcing that she spelled her name with an 'ie' rather than a 'y'. Dad laughed a lot that night and seemed very happy, though I noticed that the more he laughed, the quieter my mother became. The only thing I remember her saying was to apologize for the dinner, which she'd prepared, not realizing that we would have a guest.

Ronnie came for dinner several more times that summer. I thought Dad acted like he had a crush on her, and she *was* very pretty. I started to wonder if she really was his cousin. At twelve years old, thoughts like this had begun to occur to me for the first time.

In late August, it was time to get us kids registered for school. My parents checked out the local Catholic school but told us that with the higher rent, they could not afford the tuition. That left public school.

I was aghast that Mom and Dad would actually send us to public school with the Protestants! In the past, we had been told time and time again how fortunate we were to attend Catholic school, and how difficult it would be for the Protestants to get to heaven. This wisdom had come directly from the Sisters! When I expressed my concerns to Mom, she rose from her chair in the living room and came over to sit next to me on the couch. I noticed that her belly was getting big again.

She hugged me, looked directly into my eyes, and touched my face. "God will understand, honey." Mom further reassured me that I would be attending a brand new junior high school and would not have to walk to school anymore because a bus service was provided. But even after all of that reassurance, the prospect of attending this school both thrilled and terrified me.

I was also excited when I realized that I would no longer have to wear a uniform. Mom announced that we would all go shopping for new school clothes. On payday, my parents spent the entire check on new clothes and shoes for all of us. (I later learned that this caused us big troubles because we were unable to pay rent the following month.) They bought me three pretty dresses, two skirts, two blouses, and two pairs of shoes. Kathy and I got to pick out all of our own clothes. Mom even let me buy my first pair of nylons. I couldn't wait for school to begin so that I could show off my new clothes and meet some new friends. Even though it had been a wonderful summer, I was eager to hang out with kids my own age.

My mother was delighted that she would no longer have to pack so many lunches in the morning since the public schools had cafeterias and served lunch. She explained that we qualified for "free lunches." That detail bothered me. I wanted to know exactly how that worked. Was there a cashier in the cafeteria? Did students get tickets and mine would be given discreetly to me so that I would look like everyone else? And why did we qualify for free lunches if Dad was making so much money? I found these considerations worrisome, so I asked Mom to pack my lunch on the first day until I could figure out what I was supposed to do to get the free lunch. Mom told me that she didn't know and I should ask one of my teachers.

The night before public school started, I carefully selected a black-and-white pleated skirt with matching ruffled blouse. I even practiced putting on the garter belt and nylons, which took forever to get right. The next morning, I stood out front of our house with Kathy, Tom, Ed, and Jim to wait for the bus. My bus was different from my brothers and sisters, and I worried that I would get on the wrong one. But it turned out to be easy because the front of the bus sported a big sign that said, *Junior High*. Whew!

All of the kids on the bus chatted excitedly, but I sat there quietly because I didn't know anyone and felt very alone. Everyone was talking about who they had for "homeroom," and I fretted – I did not know how to find a homeroom. As the kids piled off the bus, I walked cautiously up to a man in a nice suit who appeared to be greeting the arriving kids. I asked him for directions to the homeroom.

"Which one?" he asked.

"Is there more than one?" I shot back, dismayed.

"Let me take a look at your schedule, young lady." I handed him the paper with my schedule printed on it. "You are in B Wing, Room 5."

Seeing my puzzled look, he kindly walked me to my classroom. Once again, the students all around me visited cheerfully, as I sat there silently feeling like a big dummy.

I did manage to figure out how to get to three more classes before the bell rang for lunch. Then I followed the stream of kids to the cafeteria. Lots of students had brought their own lunches, so I didn't feel out of place on that account. After a while, I walked into the serving area and checked out the food. Unbelievable! There were so many choices – even three kinds of desserts. I held back until most of the students were out of the kitchen, and scoped out the system: Okay, so you got a tray, put your food on it, picked up silverware, and went to the cashier to pay.

"Young lady," called the cashier, "you are going to be late if you don't make your choice and get moving!"

I walked up to her, cleared my throat, and said in a voice as low as I could. "My Mom told me that my lunch is free. So, what do I do when I pick what I want? Do I come up to you?"

"Just tell me your name, and I look at the list. Which is?" When I did not answer right away, she added, "Your name?"

"Ann Marie McCusker."

"There you are."

"Um, but just how does it work? I mean, can I only pick certain things?"

"Anything you want," she smiled, "and as much as you want, though we discourage more than one dessert."

I stood there frozen. I couldn't believe what I'd just heard, but her friendly face reassured me. "Thank you, ma'am, and I'll see you tomorrow!"

I could not wait for the next day's lunch to roll around, so I could load up. In my family, food had always been carefully portioned, and desserts had been rare until recently. This cornucopia at school seemed too good to be true.

The next morning, I bounded down the stairs, wearing my pretty new turquoise dress and my second pair of new shoes. I was surprised to find Dad sitting in his chair, unshaven, smoking a cigarette and holding a cup of coffee. Normally he would have gone to work by this time. I greeted him with a "Good morning, Dad," and found myself walking to the window to look out to where the Chevy Impala was usually parked. *Uh-oh!* I thought to myself. *No car in the driveway.*

I turned around to face my father, who said, "Don't worry honey, I have some money coming in." He held up three yellow commission slips.

"Oh, I'm not worried, Dad." And I walked out the door to catch my bus.

But I did worry. All that day. And every day for the next few weeks, until . . .

Chapter 7:

THE GRAPES OF WRATH JOURNEY

There was a spot on the highway, across from our house, where my school bus would stop to let one kid off, before turning around to drop me off.

One day, as the bus paused there, I glanced homeward and saw strangers dumping the contents of our household all over the front lawn – heaps of our clothing and furniture lying on the grass in disarray.

Before I'd had time to fully comprehend this, we were moving again. I ran full speed to the back of the school bus, gaping out the rear window.

I struggled to make sense of what I saw. My imagination ran wild. Were we being robbed? I clearly saw both of my parents standing outside *watching*, with Billy, one of my four brothers, clutching my mother's leg and crying.

The bus driver yelled for me to return to my seat, and I did so quietly, even though my heart pounded so hard that I thought it might burst out of my chest. Although completely confused, I instinctively knew that this had to be a really bad thing that was happening. *Maybe they lost the baby and had to pull everything out of the house to find her? Maybe that hole in the living room floor caved into the basement and half my family went down with it?*

Surely somebody in my family had to be injured. I'd seen little Tommy standing there, looking out at the road, crying hard. What else could have upset him so very much?

59

Yet the brief glimpse that I'd had of the worry on my mother's face had not seemed like *that* kind of worry, a kind that I'd seen many times: when one of the kids fell and got hurt, or had to be rushed to the hospital – like Jimmy, when he'd had a double hernia. For sure my mother looked upset – but not panicked.

Finally, the bus u-turned at the 7-Eleven, and I was let off at my house. Scarcely ten minutes had passed, though it had felt like an eternity.

As I leaped down the steps, my mother came up and spoke before I could. "Quickly, Ann Marie, try to find a few of your clothes and put them in the trunk of the car!"

More confused than ever, I said, "What car, Mom?" We no longer had a car. But now she pointed to an ancient car sitting in our driveway, while wordlessly handing me the baby. I cradled two-month-old Bernadine, who slept, sweetly oblivious to all that was going on.

I saw Dad and grabbed him with my free arm. "What is going on, Dad?"

His answer seemed surprisingly nonchalant. "We're moving to California."

"Why?"

"I'll explain in the car. Get moving, now!"

"I didn't know we *had* a car, Dad!"

I found a clothing pile that looked as though it had some of my stuff in it. Then I looked around for someone to hand Bernadine to. There was no one. The younger kids were just standing around, but too little to hold Bernadine; the older kids were all busy rooting through the piles. Mom held thirteen-month-old Patricia, while with her free hand carefully selecting items and putting them into a cardboard box. She was taking a picture out of its frame when Dad yelled out: "Let's go, tribe!"

And so began my family's version of a *Grapes of Wrath* trip from New Jersey to California. It was 1963.

Eleven of us squeezed into a 1950 two-door Pontiac to make the long journey: five girls, four boys, and Mom and Dad. My parents and three kids sat up front, the remaining six of us in back. As the oldest, I held Bernadine, one of the two babies in diapers. Mom was thirty years old, Dad thirty-four. I was twelve years old.

It was four in the afternoon when we headed out. We drove for about five hours, and then stopped at a diner. Dad began to look for a motel at around ten in the evening. So far, it had actually been kind of fun. This was the first time that I could remember the whole family eating dinner out. We were all surprisingly quiet, even the babies.

When we finally found a motel — and this went for the remainder of the trip, as well as that first night — we kids never went to the entrance. Dad would park the car out of sight and checked in with Mom, while the rest of us remained hidden. Once they got the room, the older kids would grab some bedding from the car trunk, and sneak inside. This worried me every time, though my mother — who is 83 years old as of this writing — *laughs* when she tells this part of the story. I did not find it funny at all. I feared that we would be found out in the middle of the night and tossed out of the room, or be forced to pay for three rooms, given there were eleven of us.

Mom and Dad would sleep on the floor, flanked by the two babies. Us three girls got one of the two beds, and the four boys slept on the other bed. For me, it was often difficult to fall asleep, sometimes because one of the babies would cry. Bernadine had an especially difficult time. It was difficult to travel with baby formula and sterilized bottles, so two-month-old Bernadine was switched from formula to whole milk. The change wreaked havoc on her little digestive system, though; she was miserable and the rest of us heard about it.

One time, I was just falling asleep when I saw Mom get up and check on each and every one of us kids, save for the two babies. She softly spoke each name like a question, starting with the boy's bed: "Tommy? Eddy? Jimmy? Billy?" Then she went to the girl's bed: "Kathy? Rosemary? Ann Marie?" When she got to me, I pretended to be asleep. I have no idea why I did, but I ended up being glad about it because then my parents began to make love. To my surprise, I felt aroused and hoped that they would do this every night. But they never did again on that trip – at least not while I was awake.

During the next few days, as our family trekked across America, we kids had a lot of questions amongst ourselves about what had happened that day, when we saw our belongings strewn across our front lawn. Finally, the oldest four of us grew bold enough to vocalize these doubts.

"Dad, what's going to happen to all of our things?" I asked.

"Don't worry," Dad replied, his voice confident. "Those guys worked for a moving company that I hired. Our belongings will most likely get to California before we do!" He laughed brightly.

"How come there was no big truck, Dad?" Tommy added.

"And no boxes to put the stuff in?" asked Kathy.

Finally, in his most sincere voice, Dad said to us, "Youse kids are not believing what I am telling you?"

"No, Dad!" "Of course not, Dad." "Sorry for asking, Dad, just wondering . . ."

We worshiped our father during those years. He was entertaining and could make just about anyone believe anything. Even if we doubted, his words touched a hopeful place in our hearts, and we always went with that hope. That ended our questions. We had no idea that we had been evicted from our home in Cherry Hill, New Jersey.

It was September, but still very hot. The old Pontiac had no air conditioning, and we were all mashed into it. Dad made at least one stop per day so that we could "refresh ourselves." This meant that we stopped at a tavern so that he could drink beer. We kids loved these stops, too, because we would each get one, sometimes two, orange sodas. Dad would give each of us a penny to put into a machine for a handful of red and white pistachio nuts. Mom, on the other hand, did not seem to like it when Dad made these stops. "We can't afford this, Tom!" she would say. To our delight, he ignored her.

One of the worst aspects of the trip was the constant stream of flat tires. It happened at least once a day, all seven of the days it took us to travel cross-country. Every time we stopped, Dad would check the severely bald tires. Every time we got gas, he put air in them. Didn't do any good. Bang! There would be another flat, and we would all pile out of the car to wait until Dad figured out how to get the tire to a gas station and back for repairs. Sometimes we would sit on the side of the road for hours until someone stopped to give Dad and the dirty tire a lift. My parents commented that folks in the southern states seemed especially kind and helpful at these times. One nice man and his wife even bought us ice cream cones while we waited for Dad to return with a mended tire.

We stopped every couple of days to do laundry, which mostly consisted of washing diapers. Most of us wore the same clothes for the entire trip. Towards the end of the journey, the car was stinky with unwashed children and their dirty clothes, but the diapers were the worst. We kids got restless, uncomfortable, and quarrelsome, but even during those times, I don't remember being scolded or hollered at. Rather, my father would suggest that we all sing a song, and taught us "California Here I Come." We'd sing it at least ten times a day, and somehow that song seemed to make everybody happy and animated, almost as "refreshed" as Dad's daily tavern stops.

One morning, Dad announced as we were driving that we would be in California by early evening of the next day. That animated the whole tribe; a cheer went up in the car. I certainly felt relief. Crammed into that back seat, I'd spent the better part of a week trying to amuse the other kids, unable to even watch the scenery slide by.

Sometimes in those days, my parents would speak in quiet, muted tones, in hopes of keeping certain things from us kids – but I could often hear parts of it and fill in the blanks. That day, I caught a whisper that we would be *entering the Mojave Desert*. There was a frightening sense of foreboding in those words and the way they were spoken. I also overheard that we were just about out of money.

We did not stop for dinner that night. Instead, my parents brought us snacks, which we devoured in the car. Long past dusk, we pulled into a motel and restaurant complex. As usual, we parked far from the entrance. But this time it was different. There wasn't enough money for a motel.

We pulled blankets from the trunk, but there were not enough to go around. The needs of the younger ones always came first, so I made a little nest for myself in the sand. It was exciting to see a tumbleweed, just like in a television western, and a huge cactus rose in the background. I watched Mom get the four youngest settled down in the seats of the car. I was just about to doze off when my father walked past, holding a beer and a huge stick, patrolling in a circle around the six of us sleeping in the sand.

"What are ya doing, Dad?"

"Just making sure youse are all safe, honey. Try to get some sleep, okay?"

"Safe from what, Dad?" He took a long swig from the beer before answering, "Snakes. Rattlesnakes are known to live in this desert."

Terrified, I silently abandoned my bed in the sand and headed for the car. Since the four youngest were in the seats, I tried to make myself comfortable on the floor. In those days, a car floor had a sizable hump right down the middle. Maybe I could curl myself into one of the three possible spots around the hump? Impossible. Stretch out with my stomach across the hump? Even worse. But I was not leaving the car. My fear of snakes then, as now, is almost phobic. So, I switched back and forth between two positions and awakened in the middle of the night to Bernadine wanting a bottle. I found it resting close to her in the driver's seat, picked her up, fed her milk, and finally fell asleep holding her.

I was not the first to awaken in the morning. Mom brought me around with a gentle tap. Everyone was busy shaking off the sand and retrieving belongings. As our tribe walked into the restaurant, the smell of bacon and sausage reminded me of how hungry I was after the previous night's dinner of saltines and peanut butter. The waitress passed out menus, but Mom quickly collected them from those of us who could read and announced that we could order cereal and that each order would need to be shared. Probably because we were all so tired, hungry, dirty, and uncomfortable, an unusual uproar occurred.

"No, I want pancakes!" "I need my own bowl of cereal!" "I am thirsty, can I order some orange juice?"

It was chaos. Kathy and I left the table to wash our faces in the restroom, knowing that we would be sharing a bowl of cereal when we got back to our seats.

Someone – maybe God, or an angel – must have overheard our distress, because a miracle happened. When Kathy and I got back to the table, we were all suddenly able to order everything and anything that we wanted, and nobody stopped us. It felt like heaven to order, then eat, two scrambled eggs, three pieces of bacon, pancakes with real maple syrup, toast, and orange juice! My stomach was so full!

A man sitting near us quietly picked up the check, after it was placed on our table. My parents thanked him.

My mother tapped this man on his shoulder as we were leaving, and said, "God bless you!" I was more grateful than embarrassed that a stranger had paid for a meal for eleven people!

65

The waitress even filled the baby's bottle with milk before we all piled back into the car. Once we were all wedged back in, our parents warned us that it would be a drive "straight through" to the Bay Area, with potty breaks only.

That last part of the ride seemed endless. Around lunchtime we finished up the last of the snacks from the night before. We all got hungry by evening but knew that there was very little money left. As I reflect about that time, I am amazed at how complacent we all were about this. Perhaps it was because we had known hunger during other lean times. There is one type of hunger that makes your stomach growl, as you think, "I have missed a meal! Food would be nice." Then there is that other hunger that goes on, and on, until the notion of food becomes an obsession. Our family knew both kinds.

Nobody wanted to sing on that final day, despite Dad's encouragement. He finally stopped asking. The only music in the car came from the soft lullabies that Mama sang to the babies. I too felt comforted to hear those familiar songs. I had heard them when I was a baby, but what I most remember is singing them myself to the four youngest – Rosemary, Billy, Patricia, and Bernadine. Towards the end of the day, there was nothing to do but try to sleep, so everyone except Dad dozed in and out until his voice snapped us all to immediate wakefulness.

"And here we are, tribe! Hayward, California. Sun all the time, and fruit that grows right in your backyard. Seems as good a place as any for our new home. So let's see if we can find a place to live."

If I was twelve years old in this day and age, an announcement like this would prompt me to say, "You have got to be kidding me! You had no flippin' idea where we were going to end up after this journey?" But it was 1963, and I had no other frame of reference than to trust that my parents would keep us safe and together. That sense of parental protection would dramatically change for me within a few years. I am glad that on that beautiful California day, I had no inkling of the hard times that lay ahead.

Dad stopped at a newsstand and picked up the local newspaper, *The Daily Review.* He flipped to the back section and read. Then he went into a phone booth and made some calls. When he returned, he announced that we would find a park for all of us to stay in for "no more than an hour," while he and Mama and the two babies looked for a house.

We were dropped off at a school with the exotic name Palma Ceia, which had a huge park and playground area. Palm trees lined the schoolyard and the streets! No one had to tell me to look after the younger kids; I automatically knew to do that. But after about half an hour, I began to worry about what I would do if my parents failed to return. Alone, in a strange place . . . what if something happened that prevented them from getting back to us? I said three Hail Marys and tossed in the Act of Contrition for good measure.

In the meantime, the kids were having fun running around, after being cooped up for so long. The weather was so agreeable, and the huge palm trees made us think about the song that we had been singing for an entire week. *California Here We Are!!!*

My parents returned a few hours later. Dad hopped out of the car with a big grin on his face. Mom looked relieved. They had found a three-bedroom house to rent, just a few blocks from Palma Ceia! They joined us kids on the grass, Dad carrying a grocery bag. He took out a beer and cracked it open, and after taking a long drink, lit a cigarette. Mom removed bread, peanut butter and jelly, and made sandwiches for us. We devoured our PB&Js but had to wait for Dad to finish his beer before we could drive to our new home on Orlando Avenue.

Suddenly, my Dad began to laugh.

"Youse kids should've seen that guy. I told him that I'd be happy to pay six months' rent in advance, just as soon as I got my pension check. I told him that I was a retired Lieutenant Colonel in the Marine Corps, but had to leave New Jersey before my check came. That a job was waiting for me and I start tomorrow, but the minute that check arrives, I will pay six months' rent. The guy did not even hesitate, he fell for my story hook, line, and sinker."

He shook his head and laughed again, snuffed out his cigarette, and finished his beer. We were all so darn proud of him! It would be years before the McCusker children could sort out this dichotomy between the values we learned in Catholic school, and the behavior of the man that we idolized.

My father was a very charismatic man – handsome, confident, and articulate. When he finally did get a job selling cars in Hayward, he always made a killing in commissions. Too bad that he could never keep a job for very long.

This was the time when I began to realize that my father had a drinking problem. Up until then, I had viewed his behavior as normal, though occasionally wondering how it was that he always managed to have beer and cigarettes even when food was scarce. But even with my dawning awareness, I could not have realized that my father was descending into alcoholism and that he would take all the rest of us down with him.

Chapter 8:

PICTURE PERFECT

I walked into the living room of our Orlando Avenue home, to find Mom taping a picture onto the wall. It was to remain the only adornment anywhere in that house for many months.

Today, deep creases cross the photograph, just as they already had on that long, bygone day. During our eviction, Mom had managed to remove it from its frame and shove it into a cardboard box, which made the journey from New Jersey with us.

From left to right: Kathy, Billy, Ann Marie (with Patricia on her lap), Rosemary, and Jimmy. The boys behind Rosemary are Tommy and Eddie.

Only eight of the nine children are in the picture, as Mom was pregnant with Bernadine at the time. It still bothers Bernadine that she's not in that picture. I used to wish that I wasn't. I still recall how much the twelve-year-old me hated that stupid 'pixie' haircut.

My family is grateful for this singular portrait of ourselves. For a long time, the picture was the only tangible evidence that we all existed prior to 1963. Over the years, relatives still on the East Coast would pass along old photos of us that they found, but none included the youngest four children.

The worn, tattered furniture visible in the photograph had seemed normal to me at the time. After months of living in an empty house in California, we finally got new furniture. Once that happened, I wanted to rip that picture off of the wall, concerned that my friends might judge me by the shabby furnishings in it.

In the picture, I hold Patricia, who is two months old. I am dead center, sitting in Dad's chair, flanked on all sides by siblings. The youngest boy is Billy, with his big bright blue eyes, sitting on the chair arm to my right. As a kid, I sometimes used to look at this photograph and think: What was to become of us all? It had certainly been a rough start. I would eventually feel blessed to have been the oldest of this "tribe," as my father called us, but that role had not been without its frustrations. Today, the photo emphasizes how central I have always been to my siblings' lives, always doing my best to fix, mend, and heal.

The house on Orlando Avenue was in the nicest neighborhood that I could have imagined living in. I was impressed with my view in the car, as we approached it for the first time, on the day of our arrival in California. The houses were all similar, yet not uniform and undistinguishable like the ones in the Projects, and much newer than our house in Cherry Hill. And every single house sported a palm tree in the front yard.

After unfolding ourselves from the cramped old Pontiac, the eleven of us descended on the house. Then the boys checked out the backyard and reported that a creek flowed by on the other side of a redwood fence. Though toting Bernadine, I made straight for the bedrooms, eager to stake out which one should be the girls' room. Accustomed to having three bedrooms, I understood that the boys would sleep in one, the girls in another, and my parents with the baby *du jour* in the smallest. I wanted the bedroom that had its very own bathroom and prepared to make my case that before long, Bernadine would be sleeping with the girls, and after all that would make five of *us* and . . .

But then I heard my mother calling me.

I found her in the kitchen, holding an empty saucepan. "Honey, the water hasn't been turned on yet. Can you please get a couple of empty milk bottles out of the car, knock on a neighbor's door, and ask them to fill it with water? I need to heat the baby's bottle, and have a bit of drinking water for the rest of us."

"Please, Mom, can you ask one of the boys to do it? I feel really uncomfortable asking a stranger for water!"

"Go. Now!" With a toss of her head, she flung her long hair aside and put one hand on her hip, striking a no-nonsense-now pose.

The advantages of being the eldest had long ceased to outweigh the disadvantages. I knew my role. Only later would I gradually become grateful for being the eldest. It would provide me with a keen sense of responsibility, and a wish to make my life different.

I found the empty bottles in the car and looked around the neighborhood. Some kids were playing across the street, so I went over and knocked on that door. Unmindful that I could have any sort of accent, I said, "The *wooder* man hasn't come to turn on our *wooder* yet, so we wondered if we could get youse to fill this up so's my Mom can heat up the bottle for the baby."

The girl who answered the door was petite, with curly blonde hair. She looked at me blankly and said, "What?" I repeated my request.

The girl turned and shouted into the house. "Mom, there's this girl at the door asking for something, but I think she's from England or something. I can't understand what she wants."

The girl's name turned out to be Vicky Podborney, and while we did not immediately become close, we were to remain friends for the rest of our lives. Later, I learned that Vicky and I were the same age and in the same grade, despite her diminutive size. She too came from a large family, although she was the middle child of eight. Vicky would soon advise me to try to get rid of my funny accent ASAP. It took about six months, but I did manage to do it.

The car was unpacked by the time I returned with the filled water bottles. My family's possessions amounted to some clothing, some bedding, and a cardboard box with a few odds and ends Mom had managed to gather. With no furniture, we piled our pillows and blankets in the living room, preparing to get our sleeping arrangement in order. I tried to make things as comfortable as possible, but worried that California might have snakes, which could slither inside houses. Although reminding myself that I was inside, and not bunking out in the Mojave Desert, I was nonetheless determined to sleep in the middle of the heap at bedtime.

Since it was still light out, we older children headed out back to hop the fence and get a better look at the creek. Redwood fences separated the residences' backyards from a culvert, where a trickle of water ran between sections of concrete pipes. The spot felt isolated, even forbidden somehow. Huge skunk cabbage grew throughout, as well as ferns and other water vegetation. My sibs and I had never seen anything like it, accustomed as we were to row after row of brick rectangular buildings. This little oasis would prove to be the source of many adventures during the time we lived on Orlando Avenue.

After surveying the creek, we tentatively went out front and sat beneath the palm tree, as dusk slowly descended upon the neighborhood. Two boys from across the street were playing catch.

We watched until one of the boys asked my brother Tom if he had a mitt and wanted to join in.

"Nope.   Don't have our furniture yet, and our baseball stuff is with that."

"Wanna play anyway?"

"Sure!"

I wished that the blonde girl – who I guessed was the boys' sister – would come out and invite me to play.

When she didn't, I went back into the empty house by myself.

Chapter 9:

CALAROGA JUNIOR HIGH

After a few days of getting settled in at Hayward, it was time for us to register for school. Dad drove us first to Palma Ceia Elementary to enroll Kathy, Tom, Ed, Jim, and Rosemary. I waited in the car for him to take me to Calaroga Junior High. None of my skirts had made it to the car in the frantic move, so I wore one of Kathy's. It was too tight around the waist and I could not button it. I had to use one of the baby's safety pins to cover the gap. It had really begun to bug me that despite my thin legs and arms, I had a thick waist. This insecurity, plus my lack of a decent wardrobe, made me even more nervous about school. I surprised myself by wishing that this school *did* require uniforms.

When Dad returned to the car I said, "Can we please go home? This skirt is so tight that it makes my stomach stick out. Plus, it's uncomfortable. Maybe I can move the button over and start school tomorrow."

I was grateful when he drove me home. Once we got there, Dad took a knife out of a kitchen drawer and cut the thread holding on the button. "Ann," he called to my mother. "Do we have a needle and thread?"

Mom emerged from their bedroom, holding Bernadine. "Tom, are you kidding me?"

"I know, not a damned pot to piss in," Dad said. He used the diaper pin, securing it in such a way that it was barely visible – still, not the fix I had hoped for. In those days, blouses were tucked in, so I had to keep pulling my blouse out enough to hide the diaper pin. Dad told me to get back into the car. "I start my new job tomorrow, Ann Marie, so we need to get all of this school business done today."

We pulled into a gas station and Dad asked where Calaroga Junior High was. Once there, we found the office and waited a few minutes to see the principal, Mr. Lopez. When he walked into the office, I instinctively rose to my feet and said, "Good morning, sir." He looked at me with a puzzled expression and then told me to have a seat. At school, I was accustomed to standing when any adult entered the room, but this formality seemed strange to the staff and students at Calaroga. Like my Jersey accent, this was another habit I would need to break.

After a short and pleasant exchange regarding my need to enroll, Mr. Lopez asked my father for my school records.

"Unfortunately, we don't have any records," said my Dad.

"This presents a problem, Mr. McCusker. Without the proper paperwork, I cannot even verify that your daughter is a seventh grader, nor do I have any idea what section to place her in. We have thirteen seventh grade classes, and each one performs at a different level. It will take weeks before her records arrive, and in the meantime, I . . . "

"That's easy," my Dad interrupted. "Put her in your smartest class. It would be a waste of everyone's time to put her with a bunch of dummies. No offense, Mr. Loupress."

"That's Lopez, L-o-p-e-z," the principal replied.

"Sorry. No offense, but my daughter has come here from one of the finest parochial schools in the country. She can give any kid here a good run for their money."

When my father bragged about me, I seldom took it as a compliment. It always felt as though he was boasting about some creation of his own, rather than about *me*. I found it embarrassing.

Even though the diaper pin gave me an extra inch at the waist, it was beginning to dig into my left side. I was uncomfortable inside and out.

After Dad left, Mr. Lopez escorted me to the counselor's office. He handed the counselor a slip of paper with '7-7' written on it in bold writing. Remembering the principal's remark that Calaroga had thirteen seventh-grade classes, I assumed that 7-7 must be the mid-level group (later I would learn that the second number had nothing to do with the level and that 7-3 was actually the brightest class). I was issued my books, PE clothing, and locker. The counselor wrote out my class schedule.

"Welcome to Calaroga, Miss McCusker," he said. "Good group of kids in 7-7. Let me see if I can find one of them to show you the ropes."

The counselor sent out a call using the intercom. "Mrs. Lindsay, we have a new student. Can you please send one of your female students to my office? I need someone who is willing to show Miss McCusker around for a few days."

I could hear static, but also lots of chattering in the background. Still accustomed to stony silence in a classroom, I took all that noise to mean that the students had been dismissed to their next class.

"Will do," replied a woman's voice. Within a few minutes, a pretty girl with big blue eyes and curly dark hair knocked on the counselor's open door. I eyed her closely from my chair. The counselor asked her to come in, and introduced her to me as "Miss Barbara Clark."

I am not sure what I was expecting, but Barbara did not seem very enthused about her assigned task. She did help me figure out how to open my locker. Barbara also made sure I knew how to get from one class to the next. But she did not invite me to sit at her table at lunch, which is what I most wanted from her. So, I devoured my lunch quickly, and then went outside to find a spot where I could stand inconspicuously by myself.

For the first two weeks at Calagora, I was lonely and kept to myself. By the beginning of the third week, I had started to get the hang of this new experience. My natural inclination to be social took over, despite my keen awareness of my shabby clothes. Barbara finally asked me if I wanted to sit with her at lunch. By the end of that week, she even suggested that maybe she could come over to my house and goof around.

Unhappily, that was absolutely out of the question. We still had no furniture, though my parents maintained the myth that our old furnishings would be arriving any day. Somehow, I managed to dodge the invitation. Finally, Barbara asked me if I would like to come over sometime for a slumber party at her house.

"You bet! Just let me know when," I said.

The following Monday, I was called into the counselor's office and told that I was being transferred to class 7-3.

"But sir, if you don't mind, I would rather stay in 7-7."

"But you must be bored in that class, and find the work too easy."

"But I have friends in that class," I said, hearing a pleading tone in my own voice.

"You'll make more friends, Ann Marie."

I felt that I would surely perish. I rebelled by going to the girls' restroom and sitting in a stall for two periods. I wanted to make a statement! However, nobody noticed my absence, and nobody came for me. That being as much disobedience as my courage would allow, I went to 7-3.

Before I even realized it, I was loving school.

There was a nice boy in my new class named Phil Cooper. We shared most of our classes together, except for P.E. and math. In our science class, Mr. Strauss assigned groups of four students to work on a project, so for a month, I got to work with Phil and two other girls. I found it hard to concentrate when Phil looked at me with those thickly lashed green eyes and felt that I acted stupid and goofy in his company. I could not imagine that a popular guy like Phil would be interested in me, but one day he said something that I have never forgotten.

We were sitting on lab seats and I had my legs crossed. I noticed that he kept looking at my legs. Finally, he leaned over to whisper in my ear, "You have the most beautiful legs I have ever seen."

No one else could possibly realize how much that comment meant to me at that moment, nor the uplift that it provided to my fragile confidence. Maybe there was more to me than drab clothing and low social standing? Being new, I was firmly at the bottom of the social ladder; most of these kids had grown up together and attended the same elementary school.

Phil already had a girlfriend, Roberta, who was very pretty and popular – so I had no illusions about being special to him. And yet a short time later, he did a second thing for which I was grateful.

Every couple of months, Calaroga held a dance for the seventh and eighth graders. The boys would stand on one side of the gym, and the girls on the other side, with those brave enough to actually dance venturing out into the middle. Phil danced exactly three times during the evening, each time a slow dance. He asked Roberta for the first and third dances, but I'll be darned if he didn't ask *me* to the floor for the second! We did not say one word to one another as we danced, but then I noticed that he and Roberta did not speak when they danced, either. I knew that he liked me but that I could not measure up to someone like Roberta. She had really cute clothes and long straight blonde hair. But I also knew that I was smarter than Roberta. Though she and I had never spoken, I knew that she was in one of the lower seventh-grade classes.

I don't remember being teased in those months when I had only two sets of clothing to wear to school, switching off skirts every other day with Kathy. More embarrassing were the days when I didn't have a lunch and had to pretend that either I had forgotten it or that I needed to diet because my skirts were too tight. These excuses must not have been very believable, because after the third or fourth time I used them, Barbara from 7-7 began to bring me a lunch each day. She did not make a big deal about it, saying only that her Mom "wanted to do it." Those lunches were amazing and always included a yummy dessert, like Twinkies. I was grateful. The other kids in my family got free lunches at their schools, but Calaroga did not serve lunch to students.

This new school offered many more activities than St. Joseph's had. One day, my English teacher, Mr. Cobble, announced that in two months the seventh-grade class would present a talent show, and he encouraged the class to put something together and audition.

After much convincing, and later down-right begging, I got three other girls to put together an act with me: Barbara, Vicky (my neighbor from across the street), and a new girl to Calaroga named Shari. We sang the Beatles tune, "I Wanna Hold Your Hand." We made three cardboard guitars, complete with glued-on strings. We tried to spiff them up with glitter, which did help a bit. Having no idea how to create a set of drums, we opted to borrow a pair of drumsticks from the band room. Barbara – I mean Ringo – planned to drum on a desk in the classroom.

When we were ready, we all went to Mr. Cobble's classroom after school to show him our act. He listened politely before saying, "Girls, everyone is doing a Beatles imitation of some kind. And one such group will most likely be chosen for the show because the students actually play instruments. But I am still proud of you all for making the effort. Thank you very much. You may go on home . . . but I would like to see you for a moment, Ann Marie."

After the other girls had left, Mr. Cobble told me that I had a beautiful singing voice and sang with great expression. He wondered if I would be interested in performing a solo. He offered to introduce me to the choir teacher after school the next day and asked me to think about it.

I had no need to think about it! I sang all the time with my family and had sung a few solos back at St. Joseph's, although those had been in Latin.

Mrs. Bennett, the choral teacher, took a keen interest in working with me. Since I did not read music, we selected a song I already knew. It was called "Aura Lee", with the same melody as Elvis Presley's "Love Me Tender." My accompaniment was Mrs. Bennett on the dulcimer, and we worked together after school two or three days a week for about twenty minutes.

A week before opening night, we were scheduled to perform a practice rehearsal in front of teachers only. We were instructed to wear our costumes or best clothes. I fretted over that, knowing that neither one of my shared skirts and blouses would be appropriate. It was pointless to ask for help from my parents, so I considered asking Barbara or Vicky if they had a dress that I could borrow. But they were both shorter than me and very skinny. I even considered backing out of the show altogether, but really didn't want to – especially because Phil Cooper was also in the show.

After a number of false starts, Barbara had finally put together a sleepover at her house that weekend. Although excited to be invited, I hoped that I wouldn't have one of my stomachache attacks, which my mother attributed to "getting ready to have my period." Plus, I wanted the chance to talk with Barb about my lack of a dress for the talent show.

I arrived on Saturday afternoon and their house seemed like a mansion to me. Barb had her own bedroom with twin beds in it. Her little brother even had his own room! We goofed around outside until dinner and then went to her room. She showed me her collection of "tiny things," which filled a whole drawer in her extra dresser – a bounty of little glass animals of every species known to the world! I had intended to ask her if she knew anyone my size who could loan me a dress, but when I saw that drawer full of lovely miniature animals, I became enviously absorbed and forgot all about my plan.

Later, we watched television and ate popcorn until bedtime. Then

Barb and I went to her room and changed into our pajamas, then hopped into our respective beds. Under my bedspread I found a blanket, and another sheet! I started to lay on top of that extra sheet when I noticed that Barb snuggled in underneath her extra. Acting as though I had done this all of my life, I copied her.

The sheets had pictures of flowers all over them; they felt crisp and clean and smelled wonderful. The pillow was not flat, but fluffy and soft. It reminded me of the motels we had stayed in while driving to California, but with eleven of us and only two beds, Mom had to divvy the motel bedding up so that everyone had something to cover up with. So on this evening, I felt more snuggly and comfortable than I ever had before, in my entire life.

Barb turned the off the light on her nightstand. Mine was still on.

"G'night, Ann Marie."

"Barb?"

"Yeah?"

"Have you noticed that I don't have a lot of clothes for school?"

"Kinda."

"Well, the moving van that was supposed to bring our furniture and clothes never showed up. So my dad has a good job selling cars, but my folks had to buy everything new and they got furniture first. Next, us kids get clothes."

"That's good."

"Yeah, but I have a problem . . . "

I went on to tell her about needing a dress for the talent show and realizing that hers would not fit me and that I didn't know what to do. Barb told me that she had a cousin about my size and would talk to her Mom in the morning. She suggested I that stay in her room when she spoke with her Mom, where I could play with her tiny things. I liked the idea of Barb speaking to her mother privately about my dilemma and hopefully switched off my own bedside light.

Barbara was not in the bedroom when I woke the next morning. After I had lounged for a few minutes in that oh-so-comfortable bed, Barb walked in. She said that her Mom had planned to cook us a hot breakfast, but had an errand to run, so was it okay with us to have cold cereal?

I was used to eating cereal, and just hoped that it was not too close to their family's payday and that they would be all out of the good cereal, like Cocoa-Puffs, and just have stuff like Corn Flakes left. But when we entered the kitchen, several boxes of cereal sat upon the table, including Sugar Pops, my second-favorite!

Barb and I munched on our cereal, giggling about how we both liked to add fresh cereal to the bowl once it began to get soggy. We heard a car pull into the driveway, and within a few minutes, Barb's dad, mom, and brother walked in. They put a box of doughnuts on the table, and I was so thrilled by such a rare treat that I didn't even notice Mrs. Clark carrying a blue dress, still on the hanger.

"Ann Marie," said Mrs. Clark, "do you think that this dress will work for the talent show?"

She held a powder-blue dress with tiny ruffles around the neckline, and a huge sash, which tied in the back. She had borrowed it from her niece, Jocelyn. Barb and I dashed to her room so that I could try it on. The fit was perfect, save for a slight resistance while zipping near the waistline. I was relieved and grateful and went on to wear the dress proudly during the shows.

Every single aspect of the three performances brought waves of happy butterflies through my whole body. I felt pretty. Phil Cooper noticed me; I saw him go to the curtain each night to watch me sing. I loved the praise and compliments I received. How could anyone possibly feel more special than I did?

And so, my world at school became a respite from the condition of my home life, and my focal point. I loved being at Calaroga. I even began to dream about having some material things that, in the past, would have been out of the question. If I got a job, if I worked hard enough, such things suddenly seemed attainable.

There were two school-related things that I really, really, *really* wanted. One was a Calaroga Leopards sweatshirt, black with a picture of our mascot on it. The other was a yearbook. The sweatshirt cost $4.50, the yearbook $8.00. At the time, spending so much money on things for myself still seemed like a pipe dream, but with my newfound confidence, I felt certain that I would find a way . . .

Chapter 10:

THE PAIN OF NO MEDICAL INSURANCE

During seventh grade, chronic stomachaches, which had been plaguing me for at least two years, started becoming more frequent. Since age ten, I had been growing a potbelly; between that and the pain, Mom thought that I must have gas or bloating issues. Now, nearly thirteen, I felt peculiar looking, with a skinny body except for my protruding stomach, and absolutely no sign of any boobs.

Barbara Clark, my first friend in junior high, moved away with her family towards the end of the school year. I missed Barbara, but luckily at about the same time started hanging out with Vicky, who lived right across the street.

Vicky had a babysitting gig most days after school. The woman for whom she babysat was young and pretty and had a collection of lovely peignoirs. We would try them on and dance throughout the house to the music of Tchaikovsky. Leaping from the couch, we imagined ourselves as beautiful ballerinas taking our bows to thunderous applause! Not only did I help Vicky babysit, I took care of the children when Vicky was too busy. Before the end of the school year, I had earned enough money to buy that school sweatshirt and yearbook!

Vicky used her babysitting money to buy the coolest new outfit: pink with bell-bottomed hip huggers and a short baby-doll blouse. An outfit like that would have looked awful on me with my protruding belly, and I was envious.

One afternoon as I babysat with Vicky, I had one of the worst stomach cramps so far. I doubled over, fell to the floor, and could not get up. Vicky ran across the street to my house and returned with my father, who was 'not working' that day. Dad had to carry me home, as I cried out in agony. Within a few moments, the pain eased and I felt fine. But that episode finally got the attention of my parents, who took me to St. Rose Hospital that same day. Mom and I walked the eight or so blocks and checked in with Emergency.

The doctor carefully checked my abdomen, and then asked me to stand and bend forward. When I did, he grabbed my stomach. Instinctively, I sucked in my gut. He told my mother that he would need to do a pelvic exam. I had no idea what that entailed, but got the notion once I laid back on the table – he asked me to put my feet in the stirrups and open my legs. My initial feeling of utter embarrassment was quickly superseded by pain, as he put some instrument into my private area.

My mother was standing across the room when the doctor said, "Mrs. McCusker, your daughter is pregnant."

I knew that was completely impossible and to my mother's credit, she immediately agreed. The doctor launched into lecture her about how little parents sometimes know, but my mother would have none of it. Finally, he requested an x-ray.

The result showed a large mass attached to my right ovary. The doctor recommended that I be admitted immediately. As I was taken to the pediatrics floor, my mother went to an office to speak with the admitting department.

But mere minutes later, Mom walked into the ward with my clothing and told me that we were going home. St. Rose was a private Catholic hospital in Hayward, and since my parents had no insurance to pay for surgery, I had been referred to the county hospital in Oakland.

Two days later, Mom and I took the bus twenty miles to Highland Hospital, where I was mortified to be put through yet another pelvic examination. After that ordeal, my surgery was scheduled for May 16th – just three days after my thirteenth birthday.

I guess the admitting folks had not realized that by the time of my surgery, I would be an adult by hospital standards, so they gave Mom and me a tour of the children's ward. The area seemed cozy and comforting, with stuffed animals everywhere, plus lots of toys, which naturally seemed ridiculously juvenile to me. Many of the children were in cribs, but there were also many regular beds, and we saw a couple of kids around my age. Though wishing that I could be at St. Rose, I managed to convince myself that maybe this wouldn't be *so* bad.

Between that first diagnostic appointment at St. Rose and my check-in date at Highland, Dad got a new job selling cars. He was able to drive me to the hospital in his brand-new Chevy 'demo'. When we arrived, we were directed to the adult ward, not the children's ward. Of course, I had prepared myself for something entirely different, but apparently, since our tour, the hospital staff had realized that I had turned thirteen.

The adult women's ward consisted of a single room with long rows of beds and some two dozen or so patients. In those days, a level of racial segregation still existed – two beds in the corner, with the only window, were sectioned off by a screen for me and the only other white patient.

Dad kissed me goodbye and assured me that he and Mama would visit me the next day after my surgery.

I had a look around. The ward had no telephones or television. There was a card table with a few jigsaw puzzles, but those were of no interest to me. Then a black nurse came in and handed me a hospital gown. She asked me to put it on and meet her in the lavatory for my 'shave'. I wondered if I was going to have my head shaved. Maybe I needed to have electrodes on my head to keep track of something?

I changed into the gown and asked at a nurse's station for directions. The lavatory consisted of several toilet stalls and tiled shower facilities. When I walked in, the nurse was waiting for me, holding a razor in one hand, a towel and shaving cream in the other. She directed me to one of the stalls and said, "Okay, spread them long legs, honey."

I was shocked, but managed to stammer, "Ah, let's see. Where are you, I mean, are you thinking about shaving me, uh, well, like, down there?"

"Where's else was you thinking I'd be a shavin' you, girl?"

"I see, but, I guess, it is just that it may not be necessary. I, uh, well, I just don't have any hair down there yet."

She lifted my hospital gown and took a peek. "I sees what you mean. Okay, we can skip this so you just go on back to your ward, okay?" Grateful and relieved, I returned to my bed.

The woman next to me was about my mother's age and had just returned from surgery. She lay awake and moaning. I couldn't think of anything to say to her, though I wanted to provide comforting conversation. Thank God I was able to busy myself with my liquid dinner tray, which provided me with green Jell-O, soup with nothing in it, and some apple juice. I ate quickly and wondered what I could do next to keep myself occupied. It was only 5:30 P.M.

I couldn't see the patients on the other side of the screen, but I heard them. There was so much moaning and crying that I began to be afraid. A woman came in with a clipboard and told me that she needed to ask some questions. "Do you have any allergies? Is there any cancer in your family?"

Cancer? Now, I wondered if I was about to die. How had I forgotten to pack my rosary beads? I wanted my mother but my family had no phone. Still, I desperately needed to talk to someone. I pushed the call button, and when the nurse came, I told her that I needed to speak with my doctor right away. She could see that I was holding back tears and shaking. The nurse agreed to have him paged.

She returned about twenty minutes later and said, "He's gone home."

At this, I burst into tears. All I could manage to say was, "I am so very, very scared." I will never forget that nurse's kindness. She called my doctor at home, and he appeared about an hour later.

My young doctor was doing his residency at Highland. He was probably sleep deprived. Judging from the look on his face, he wasn't very happy about being called back to the hospital. In a stern voice, he asked, "Just what can I do for you, Miss McCusker?"

Not the type of kid for whom tears came easily, I set a personal record that night. All I could manage to get out between sobs was, "I want to go home!"

Gratefully, the doctor's tone softened and he talked to me about "fear of the unknown." I did not find his words particularly comforting, but I was very happy to at least not be alone with my thoughts.

The doctor instructed the nurse to bring me a "sleeper," which I did not realize was a pill until she returned and handed one to me with a small cup of water.

"We both have to get up very early tomorrow and get you taken care of, but I will sit with you until you begin to get drowsy," said the doctor.

We chatted about school. I started to think about what a nice man he was and felt myself getting a crush on him. It was not his looks, but his compassion, which drew me to him. I asked if he was married, and felt disappointed when he said that he was. He then asked me if I thought that I would like to have children one day.

"Heck, no!"

"And why is that?"

"Mom says that when the baby comes out, they have to cut you down there to make space for the baby to get through."

"Ah, you don't even feel that part. Your body naturally numbs itself. I must say that after delivering a number of babies, I have not heard a complaint."

I began to blink heavily.

"Okay, princess, see you in the morning."

I fell off to sleep comforted.

I vaguely remember a nurse inserting an IV into my arm the next morning, and putting a cap over my hair. My next memory was awakening to see the doctor sitting by my side and I was back in the ward. My parents had not yet arrived, so the doctor explained to me what had happened during the four-hour surgery.

The tumor was not cancerous, but it was big – weighed five and a half pounds, and had been attached to my right ovary and fallopian tube. He explained that tumors send out "feelers," and that these had been everywhere. The feelers had to be removed one strand at a time. Due to the tumor's progress, it had been necessary to remove my right ovary and fallopian tube, along with three-quarters of my left ovary. That one-quarter of an ovary, the doctor explained, would still release an egg every month. "Just in case you change your mind about having children one day," he said, smiling. He seemed happy about that, so I smiled back. The last thing I remember from that conversation was the doctor telling me that he would give me something for the pain, and it would make me sleep.

The next time I awoke, it was to the sound of someone calling my name. I opened my eyes to see Mom and Dad standing at the foot of my bed. I was so happy to see them, and apparently blurted out, "It weighed five and a half pounds!" Both my parents turned crimson and looked around the room. My Dad turned his head over to the other patient in our corner and said, "It was a tumor, not a, uh, well, never mind."

Later that night, Barbara Clark and her mom came to see me, bringing me a box of See's chocolates and a card with a five-dollar bill in it!

The next day, the nurse got me up to walk, which really hurt, but within a few seconds, I was more focused on how thin I felt. My potbelly was suddenly almost gone, and it felt as though my stomach matched the rest of my body. This made me very happy. Maybe no more troubles zipping and buttoning anything around my waist? I smiled inwardly, remembering the safety pin I'd used to clasp my skirt on that first day at Calaroga. It felt like years since anything had fit me properly. I made a mental note to ask the doctor how long he thought this tumor had been growing inside me.

After a couple of recovery days in that dreary ward, the boredom really set in. It seemed as if every minute dragged on endlessly. I couldn't call anyone and never knew if or when someone would come to visit. To my surprise, one evening my parents showed up with my buddies Vicky and Shari. To this day, both of these women remain important friends. Now, as then, Vicky had a contagious laugh and managed to find humor in everything. During her visit, I found myself begging her to stop making me laugh. I had stitches across my stomach, and it hurt so much. Yet it also felt wonderful and healing.

Highland Hospital was in the steep terrain of the Oakland hills, and from my window I could see the hospital entrance. To combat my boredom, I would watch people climb and descend the several flights of narrow concrete steps down there. After my parents, Shari, and Vicky left the hospital, I waited with my window open to call to them as they descended those steps. Catching sight of them, I shouted, "I love you all so much! Thank you for coming to visit me!"

When Shari heard me, she turned and lost her footing. She stumbled and slid down at least a dozen steps on her butt. My father ran to her and apparently determined that she was okay because I could see him starting to laugh. Shari stood and began rubbing her bottom. I could hear Vicky laughing, and then I found myself consumed by giggles. My stitches felt as though they were breaking free, but I couldn't stop. I waved and closed the window, and worried that I'd probably peed a little.

My nice young doctor came to see me every day, and each time I asked when I could go home. He had already told me that I would need to stay for at least five days, and maybe seven or eight. At the end of the fourth day, I asked if I could go home tomorrow. He responded with, "You have a temperature, Ann Marie. It needs to come down a bit before you can be discharged."

I so wished to be at St. Rose so that my friends and family could simply walk to see me – if only we had had medical insurance. I hated this place; even the grouchy woman in the bed next to me had been discharged, leaving me more alone. The only thing I had to look forward to were the three hot meals delivered right to my bed each day. At least, I reassured myself, I didn't have cancer, as the woman next to me had learned. I would survive.

On the sixth day, I still had a temperature. When the doctor came to check on me, I did my best begging job, pleading with him to allow me to go home. I was delighted when he agreed, though he told me that he would send me home with antibiotics, just in case the fever meant that my body was battling an infection. Also, he wanted to see me in two weeks.

At first, I was excited to be going home. But as I put on my clothes and waited for my dad to pick me up, I suddenly felt trepidation. I reflected upon what I was going home to. Remembering . . .

Mom had eleven pregnancies in twelve years. After the first five children were born, our family lacked any health insurance. I now understood the danger of that situation, in a way, I never had in the past. My Mom and the last six babies had received no prenatal care. Had this contributed to the fact that two of my brothers had died shortly after birth?

Mom's pregnancies had taken a toll on her appearance. She looked worn out. Her once thick and shiny hair had become long and stringy. She had a couple of missing teeth and we couldn't afford dental care. After several evening beers, my Dad would berate her. I suffered for her when he called her "fat and toothless." We children were overcome with confusion and fear by such words, and no one dared speak one word of retort during these tirades. Occasionally in a courageous moment, my mother would reply, "You made me this way." I remember thinking, *Go Mom! Fight back for once!*

On occasion, Dad had added the word "whore" to these accusations. I was stunned and shocked, even though only vaguely aware of what that word meant. Of course, such allegations could not be true, so had my father lost his mind? What possessed him to be so cruel? The answer came to me when I realized that he was only mean when he was drinking. At that point, I still knew little about the disease of alcoholism.

Gutless as we all were, none of us would dream of confronting our Dad. We mirrored how Mama handled it, which meant simply being grateful when he was working and there was food in the house. Dad sold cars exclusively on commission, so we had months of financial normalcy, followed by months of slim pickings. Gradually, the pattern became clear to me. When Dad was not making money, his abuse of my mother resurfaced. Was he projecting anger and embarrassment onto my mother about his own failures to provide for us? Regardless, during such times, we all stepped quietly throughout the house, lest some disturbance set him off, and I spent as little time there as I possibly could. Though I was able to escape, doing so tugged at my heart for the little ones who were not yet in school, and stuck at home.

My four sisters and I slept in the same bedroom. It was the master bedroom, so we had our own bathroom. Kathy and I slept in bunk beds, while Rosemary and Patricia shared a twin bed, and Bernadine had her crib. After we all went to bed, we could hear Dad start in. I would become hyper-vigilant, my ears straining to listen and make sure that Mom was okay. My sisters would lie tense and silent in their beds, saying nothing, but I knew that they, too, were wide awake. Sometimes I would hop down from the top bunk, and find their eyes open. I would scoop up toddler Patricia and baby Bernadine and put them in my bed, and hold them.

And was all of that what I really yearned for, instead of being safe and well fed in the hospital? Yeah, I guess it was, if only for my siblings' sake . . .

Both of my parents arrived to pick me up from the hospital. This worried me, as it meant that Kathy, only eleven years old, had been left alone to watch our seven other siblings. I said not a word to my parents, rationalizing that we would be home soon.

But my precarious sense of comfort dissipated the moment that I walked in the door of our home.

Boxes lay everywhere. The house was a chaotic mess. How had I not seen the signs before I'd left for my surgery? First, the newspaper had stopped, and then the garbage service. For months, we had been stacking the garbage bags in the garage, which reeked. Then the television, and later some smaller appliances like the toaster had disappeared, all sold to a second-hand store. None of this had been remarked on by any of us in the family, as we knew that it meant that finances were very tight. But did it mean we were moving? Again?

Neither Dad nor Mom had mentioned a word about this on our drive home from the hospital. Instead, my mother asked my dad if the hospital had agreed to send me home with my prescriptions and bill us for the cost (in addition to pain medication and antibiotics, the doctor had explained that I would need to take estrogen for six months, as my reproductive system had been "seriously interrupted"). Dad had shaken his head no.

Now, I knew why. Despite the fact that he had a new job, we were too far behind to catch up on bills, and he probably had not yet received a paycheck. Dad wanted us to make yet another a fresh start in yet another home. In short, we were once again evicted.

My stomach hurt.

Chapter 11:

CLIFFWOOD AVENUE

When we reminisce about our childhoods, my siblings and I still 'tell time' by the houses we lived in. Between 1963 and 1967 we moved to five different houses: Orlando Avenue, Fleetwood Drive, Manon Avenue, Cliffwood Avenue, and Coronado Street. If you spoke with my siblings today, you would witness a subtle shadow cross our faces when we refer to *Cliffwood Avenue,* a name which evokes troubled times and bad memories. On Cliffwood, our lives became a nightmare.

I entered my sophomore year in high school when we moved to Cliffwood Avenue in 1966. School would become my place of sanctuary and respite for the next three years. At the end of my freshman year, I had snagged a summer job working as a custodian's assistant at the high school, and in the evening, I babysat for a single mom who worked at night. For the first time, I had my own money! I stepped up my wardrobe. I bought outfits for Trish and Bernadine. I bought slipcovers to hide the tattered furniture. Rosemary remembers that I threw her a party for her eighth birthday – it was the only birthday party that any of us had ever had. And I purchased food – lots of it. My monthly paychecks of $156.00 from the high school, and $75.00 from babysitting went a long way in those days.

The sense that I was responsible for the well-being of my siblings had taken root long before, but it began to blossom in 1966. I had long been present for emotional support, but once I worked, I did everything in my power to use my financial resources to create some sense of normalcy in our continuously degenerating household.

As I grew older it became ever clearer to me that our family suffered because my father was an alcoholic. This disease was not discussed much in those days. My father's problem was dismissed as 'an Irishman liking his beer'. He'd never managed to hold down a job for any length of time after getting booted from the police force in Woodbury; alcohol was the primary culprit, and his joblessness had begun to feel normal.

Along with this budding awareness, a new thought began to haunt me: Why wasn't my mother doing anything about our family struggle? Uncle Joe, my father's older brother, had moved to Hayward the year before. Now, Dad had a drinking buddy. Joe's wife of seventeen years finally had enough, refusing to put up with his antics, abuse, and unstable financial support. Aunt Carol, and my two cousins, Michael and Patrick, packed up and left, and I never saw them again. I wondered – why couldn't my mother muster up the strength to do likewise?

But then again, Aunt Carol had only two children. Mom had lots of little ones in the house. I wondered if things might change for the better, for all of us, if she would only stand up to him. But we were all afraid of him. All I could do was put such thoughts aside and deal with the problems at home as they arose.

At this time, Dad's verbal abuse became more threatening. He would sometimes chase my mama through the house, shouting that he was going to kill her. This always occurred at night, after we children went to bed. His rage seemed to be escalating, and I became sick with worry that he really would harm my mother. Many a night, I jumped out of the bathroom window and ran in my pajamas to the nearest phone booth – gratefully, only a few blocks away – to call the police. And every time the police arrived, all they did was to tell Dad to go to bed and sleep it off.

After at least half a dozen times through this cycle, I began to wonder if there was any way to end this nightmare. All of our relatives lived on the East Coast, and I considered calling one of them, particularly my Aunt Dean, who seemed to have some power over her brother. But I didn't and went about my life feeling powerless.

Most mornings after such episodes, Dad couldn't remember the late-night police visits, so there were no repercussions. But one morning he *did* remember the police arriving and realized that it must have been me who had called them. My punishment awaited me when I arrived home from school that afternoon. He had burned every scrap of my clothing in a backyard burn can that morning. Not sure if Kathy had been involved, he went ahead and burned her clothes as well. By the time Kathy and I walked in the door, he was already fretting with remorse and apologized. Out of fear we feigned forgiveness, knowing that the night was young and an eternity of evening hours lay ahead.

Sure enough, I awoke in the night to his loud voice. Normally, my mother's replies were hushed and barely audible. This time, I could hear her voice even over my father's ranting. She was calling for help! I bolted upright on my top bunk bed, noticing that my four sisters were also sitting up. And then I heard Mom cry, "Ann Marie, help me!"

I wish I could say that I bounded out of bed and ran to the living room. But I did not. I told my sisters to stay where they were, and with every muscle in my body shaking, walked slowly and tentatively into the living room.

There was a freestanding fireplace there, which separated the living room and kitchen. I found Mom running around and around it, with Dad in pursuit. She saw me and stopped, out of breath and panting. Dad made the most of that delay. He clenched his left fist and struck her full-force on the right side of her mouth.

Blood squirted everywhere. Mom put her hand to her bloody lips and said, "You bastard!"

My Dad said nothing. He slowly walked to their bedroom, went in, and closed the door behind him.

I heard crying coming from both the boys' and girls' bedrooms. I wanted to go to the children and reassure them, but Mama's bloody mouth demanded my attention. I grabbed a dishtowel from the sink and handed it to her.

"Let's go, Mama. You need to go to the hospital."

Kaiser was only three blocks from our home. Mama and I walked there in our pajamas. By the time we arrived, the dishtowel was soaked with blood, as was her nightgown. The emergency staff hurried her to a room, and I was told to wait outside. Soon I noticed the police going into her room, so I went in, too.

"Mrs. McCusker, you need to press charges," one of the policemen said. "That is the only way we can help you."

"You don't understand," my mother muttered through her swollen lip. She was barely able to speak. She glanced at me, then back to the police officers, and told them that she wanted me to leave the room. I did so without complaint, but not before shouting to the officers, "Check your records and see how many times you have been called to our house! Can't you please help us?"

I sat on a plastic chair in the waiting room, hoping we could leave before sunrise. I didn't want any of my friends or neighbors to see my mother and me walking home in bloodstained pajamas. After about half an hour, the police left and my mother came out. She'd had thirteen stitches, and held an ice pack to her mouth. She looked so miserable; I could only hug her. All I wanted to do was comfort her.

But on the walk home, I felt anger surging through my veins. I consciously tried to quiet my voice so that I could ask her a question without letting her know how livid I felt. Somehow it came out like a whisper.

"Are you going to have him arrested, Mom?"

"No, Annie. That would just make it worse, and you know that he will be okay in the morning."

When she said that, the rage that I felt made me feel like throwing up. I realized that I was as angry at *her* as I was with my Dad. But as I looked at her face, and my heart softened again: stitches, blood oozing through the bandage, her voice a bit slurry from swelling and pain medication. She simply said, "Please, Ann Marie."

With clarity unknown to me until that very moment, I realized that my mother was never going to do anything.

The remainder of the walk home was silent between my mother and me. I longed to be able to talk with someone outside the family about this, but would have been too embarrassed. These things were simply not much discussed in those days.

When we got home, the house was quiet, the sun just beginning to shed its light into the window by my top bunk. I removed my bloodied pajamas, put on a fresh nightgown, and debated whether I should try to get an hour of sleep, or just get ready for school. I looked up to my bunk, and found Rosemary and Patricia up there, fast asleep and each hugging one of the stuffed animals I used to adorn my Spartan room. So, I went to the shower, readying myself for the one place where I could pretend to be a normal teenager.

I missed my friend Vicky, who had recently moved along with her family to Dublin, California. But I still had Shari. One day, as we were walking from my house to hers, a Jeep pulled up to the curb. The two boys in it were seniors at Mount Eden High School, and I recognized them immediately – Steve DuPont and Derekard Ricci were among the cutest boys in the school and very popular. "How about a ride, girls?" they asked.

Now, Shari and I were both considered 'good girls'; even though she was quite pretty and always attracted attention from boys, she was also shy and conservative. But on this day, I was also feeling particularly attractive, in part, because I was not suffering from a zit outbreak. So, before Shari could decline, I blurted out, "You bet!" Shari appeared hesitant, but as we approached the jeep I whispered to her, "Please, Shari, do this for me."

We hopped into the backseat of the roofless Jeep. Steve drove us into an abandoned apple orchard, where he swerved the Jeep around wildly, weaving in and out amongst the trees. It was such a thrill – I enjoyed every minute. Then the boys took us out for a Coke, and their manner became more subdued. I wondered if they had lost interest in us. Shari and I muse together to this day that back then we were 'as pure as driven snow' – in other words, virgins, and not in any way ready to change that status, despite the 'free love' that was becoming vogue right there in California.

Derek, the one who caught my eye, did mention during this outing that he was taking karate at Gaylord's in downtown Hayward. Martial arts were just becoming popular at the time, and while he clearly said this to impress us, my mental wheels began to turn. Here was the tall, dark and handsome man of my fantasies, with a dimpled chin and charming demeanor to boot. If I signed up at Gaylord's, I could not only see him but also learn to defend myself. Maybe even learn to defend my mother.

Derek lived a few blocks from our house on Cliffwood, and I often saw him walking to school, but had never dreamed of speaking to him. After our Jeep ride, I started timing my walks to school to coincide with his, although he barely managed to make it on time. I would peep out my front window, waiting for him to pass, willing to risk being late for school. When I saw him approach across the street, I would *just happen* to be leaving at the same time. During several of these shared walks to school, we spoke about his karate lessons, although I neglected to mention that I was saving up for my own. That $6.00 cost me dearly, too, because I still needed to replace my wardrobe after my father's act of arson.

When I arrived finally at Gaylord's as a paying student, on a Thursday evening at 7 P.M., I was dismayed to learn that the girls' and boys' lessons were conducted separately. Mine would be after his, at 8:00. While disappointed, I assured myself that at least Derek and I would now have more common ground for conversation during our walks to school. Perhaps after I got better, Derek and I could even practice together. I worked hard at my lessons to make that a possibility.

Unfortunately, Derek dropped out of his lessons after three months – but I went on to take karate for three more years, and eventually became one of the instructors for the girls' class. Later, I was invited to join the school's coveted exhibition team, which gave demonstrations. It was a proud yet scary moment for me when my karate school gave a demonstration at Mount Eden High during an assembly. Bundle of nerves that I was going into that event, my usual control went out the window. I must have practiced that kick a dozen times on my 'dummy' assailant – but when it came time to perform in front of all my classmates, I kicked my fellow student Felix so hard in the groin that he went down. And stayed down. The crowd in the gymnasium burst into applause. I followed the protocol drilled into us karate students and bowed. Mr. Gaylord came toward me, bowed, and whispered, "Get your ass out of here, and get in the van with Felix." Poor Felix could only hobble out the door, having to lean on me to walk. Perhaps the crowd thought that was part of the act, too, because they stood to their feet, cheering and applauding.

Though Felix had been wearing the required protective cup (those stinky, gross contraptions that the boys left all over the changing room), he was hurt badly enough that he later had to go to the hospital. I was put on a two-week suspension from the team.

Derek had witnessed the whole thing from his seat in the bleachers. The next time we walked to school together, he teased me about "demasculinizing" poor Felix.

As with my junior-high crush, Phil Cooper, Derek already had a girlfriend. Her name was Shirley Billings and she was a beautiful, curvy, and popular junior. Every guy at Mount Eden wanted to date her. As for me: No boobs yet . . . horrible wardrobe . . . unfashionably curly hair that I had to iron each morning to get that straight look . . . and worst of all, a reputation for being a 'nice girl' and a 'brain.' I had no chance and felt doomed to be the kind of girl whom guys just wanted to be friends with. This was one of the few times in my life when I wished to be more like my sister Kathy. Flirting seemed so natural and easy for her.

Derek did seem to enjoy my company. Over Christmas, he invited me to go to Midnight Mass with him and his family. I agreed, but fretted over what to wear, given that my entire wardrobe had been burned up. I managed to find a summer dress on sale, which was sleeveless but did have some red embroidery at the bottom. I figured that if I wore a sweater over it, he would never suspect that I'd only paid $3.00 for it.

I'd hoped to meet him outside my house at our designated time, 11:30 PM. I didn't want him to see that my family had no Christmas decorations to speak of that year – not even a tree. Plus, there was no telling what condition my Dad might be in. Derek knocked on the door at 11:15 PM, but thank God I was ready and there in a flash! I was just sliding out the door when my Dad bellowed, "Hey, I want to meet this guy!" I pretended not to hear him and shut the door.

Over spring break, Derek popped over one afternoon to see if I wanted to take a walk. When I greeted him at the door, he said that he had something he wanted to talk with me about. I invited him in and introduced him to my parents. When I excused myself to retrieve my jacket, my father said, "Just a minute. Both of you! I have something that I want to ask in front of both of you."

He told the children who were present to empty out. Silently, the few who were in the living room went out the front door. I knew this was not going to be good and prayed that it would not be horrible.

It was horrible.

"I just have one question for you, Derek."

"Yes, sir."

"Are you having an affair with my daughter?"

"No sir, I am not."

"Better not be!" boomed my Dad.

"Yes, sir, I mean no, sir. We are strictly just friends."

Sick creep, I wish you were dead! Is what I thought. "Dad, stop it!" is what I said, holding my hands up.

Later, I wondered why I'd done that – holding up my hands up, a gesture that suggested surrender, instead of screaming at him. I supposed that I must have hoped to ward off later reprisals. And I found myself doing what we all did in our family – acting later on as though it had never happened.

At that moment, though, I felt ready to die from embarrassment and shame. I don't remember exactly what happened next, but Derek and I somehow managed to leave the house. My only comfort was that at least this had happened in the afternoon. If it'd been in the evening my father would have been drunk and his words probably far more disgusting. I was not sure what part of what I'd just heard was worse: my father's accusations or Derek declaring that we were "strictly friends."

Derek and I were walking away down the street when he put his hand on the back of my neck and said, "Don't worry about this. Looks like you've got a lot on your plate there, Annie. Parents can be such jerks. I know that myself first hand."

I felt grateful for his understanding – and his willingness to let this mortifying issue slide.

Derek and I continued to walk to school together for the remainder of the school year but never again discussed my family issues. He also never set foot in my home again.

At around this time, rumors were swirling around Mount Eden that Derek's girlfriend, Shirley, was pregnant. I eyed her with care and envy every time we passed in the hallway. I did notice that she appeared to be gaining weight. And then one day, she disappeared from school altogether. I suspected at the time that this was what Derek had wanted to discuss with me that day before my father's sick accusation spoiled the mood. As things turned out, he never did discuss her pregnancy with me.

Derek and his family were to play a rather significant role in my life, but that was still about a year in the future. It would not involve the role of girlfriend that I dreamed about, but it would provide me with comfort.

Shortly after Dad embarrassed me in front of Derek, Shari announced that her family was moving to Fremont, California. We both became very emotional over this. The year before, we had been a trio, until Vicky had moved away. Now, Shari and I were virtually inseparable. Each of us was terrified of losing the other. We decided to plot out how we could manage to live on our own – both of us detested our home lives anyway. We considered running away and sleeping each night in the camping gear section of the local Sears store. Or perhaps Mr. Gaylord would allow us to sleep at the karate school. Either way, we could shower each morning at the high school.

But when the time came, we simply shared tearful goodbyes. Although Fremont was a scant fifteen miles from Hayward, it might as well have been fifteen thousand miles since we didn't have any way to get together.

For a while, I went without a close friend to hang out with at school. Socializing with my sister, Kathy, was not an option. Over the past two years, we had chosen very different paths. Two distinct social groups had become known at Mount Eden: the *surfers* and the *hoods*. While I belonged to neither, Kathy was clearly a hood. She teased her hair to unfathomable heights, wore lots of make-up, blew off school, and smoked cigarettes. She was quite a beauty, which afforded her status with the girls in her group – but I wanted nothing to do with her in public.

One day in late spring, I was at my locker in A Wing at the end of school, shoving some books in and getting others out for the evening's homework assignments. A young hood, that I recognized slightly, tapped me on the shoulder and said, "The Mexican chicas are beating the shit outa your sister."

"Where?"

"Right out there." She pointed to the grassy area just outside of A-Wing.

I flew out the double doors to find three girls encircling Kathy. One pulled her hair, and another yanked at her ear, as if hoping to rip out her dangling earring.

I dropped my books. A feeling swelled up inside, which reminded me of the time I'd punched Linda Gayle in elementary school, and my karate training took over. The girl behind my sister, who was yanking Kathy's hair, had her face completely exposed to me. I gave the girl a strong forward punch from my right fist. That left me slightly off balance, but I managed to recover some level of stance and deliver a right sidekick to the bitch pulling Kathy's earring. Then I made menacing eye contact with the third girl. With a little help from Kathy, they all took off.

My sister and I crumbled into one another's arms.

Her face was scratched and her ear was bleeding, though her earring was still intact. She recovered her composure in a heartbeat because suddenly we had a crowd around us. Her face resumed the hard look, which had become so familiar to me that year.

"You better run you bitches!" screamed my sister. "Too chicken to meet me one-on-one! Cuz you know I'd beat your ass!" And then, Kathy and I walked home together from Mount Eden High, for the first and last time.

✳✳✳ ✳✳✳ ✳✳✳

Looking back on these long-ago years, I often find it helpful to compare my memories with those of my siblings. Two of my sisters, Kathy and Rosemary, live in the same town as I do (Corvallis, Oregon).

Rosemary, eight years my junior, recalls strong impressions of fear from Cliffwood – lying awake at night, listening to our father rant. Rosemary and Patricia shared a twin bed and they often cuddled together, becoming even more terrified if the situation seemed to demand my presence, as the eldest. Rosemary recently said to me, "That's when I knew it was bad, Ann Marie . . . when you got up. When you had the courage to go into that living room!"

Kathy reminded me that Mom's face injury had required so many stitches because Dad had a cast on his hand and wrist at the time. This was because he had earlier punched the brick wall above the fireplace in a desperate act of frustration. I'd forgotten about the cast. She views Cliffwood as where the stress of being unable to support such a large family, finally made something snap in our father. Kathy claims that he had a nervous breakdown – as if that excuses his violent behavior. Kathy also remembers that at Cliffwood, Dad switched from drinking beer to cheap wine, and that seemed to make him more violent.

I remain astonished by what a forgiving bunch we all have been. Dad was always tearfully remorseful over his bad behavior, which made it easier to pardon; meanwhile, the rest of us developed a high tolerance for dysfunction. But at least some of our forgiveness at the time stemmed from the fact that we were just plain *scared* of this Jekyll-and-Hyde man with whom we had to live.

Chapter 12:

DEFENDING MY FAMILY

There was a girl in my karate class, Terri Cook, who was also a sophomore at Mt. Eden. I thought she was weird, at first. Her mouth was full of metal. In 1967 it was definitely not helpful to one's reputation to wear braces. Terri did have long, glossy, straight hair, which was a big plus. But the way she moved her head added to the weirdness. If she wished to turn her head, she never used her neck. She turned her entire body. I realized that this was an effort not to mess up her hair.

I was friendly to Terri during karate lessons, though not particularly interested in socializing with her at school. But then Shari moved, leaving me with no one. At that point, Terri and I began to hang out at Mt. Eden, and another girl with braces joined in to make us a trio. The third girl's name was Pam Donohue. Terri and Pam both came from 'normal' homes, so initially, I told them little about my own home life. I just said that we had some "family problems."

Later, a girl named Gail also joined our group. As the only extrovert, I made most of the group decisions, and managed to talk the three introverts into trying activities outside their comfort zones – nothing abnormal, just stuff like going to dances, and cruising the strip around the karate school on a Friday or Saturday night. Terri's parents purchased a car to be shared amongst the three teenage drivers in their household. It was a blue Chevy Impala, and for the first time, a group I was part of had wheels! I took advantage of this to stay away from home as much as possible, spending the night with one or another of these friends as often as I was invited. (Kathy remembers feeling abandoned when I did this, recently telling me, "I didn't like being the oldest when you were gone.")

During the evenings when I was at home, we would all watch television as Dad sat in his chair drinking wine and smoking cigarettes. Other than that one chair, the only place to sit in the living room was on the couch, which we older ones gave up to the little ones. Kathy, Tom, Ed, Jim, and I found places on the floor, especially if one of our favorite TV shows was on, like *Bonanza*.

One evening, Dad complained that I was blocking his view of the TV. We were all polite, respectful children for the most part, but this time the nearly sixteen me sassed him back, suggesting that maybe it was someone else's turn for his chair and he could sit on the floor like the rest of us. By then he had enough wine in his system that he took this as a challenge.

"Okay, you little smart ass. Ever since you started taking the goddamned karate you think you are a tough shit, don't you?"

All eyes widened and looked to me. I told myself to apologize – let him win and avoid a conflict that would upset everyone. This was the first time I could remember him swearing at any of us children. Fear gripped my heart. But there was also something else inside of me, which I recognized as boiling rage.

"I've learned a lot in karate, Dad."

"So show me!"

I slowly rose to my feet. My heart raced as the fight-or-flight instinct took over. I didn't want to run, so my choice was clear.

"Stop it, Tom," came my mother's voice.

"It's okay, Mama. I am just going to show him a trick I learned on the exhibition team." I hoped to make it all seem like a demonstration, almost playful. That's what I wanted my family to think. But inside, in my gut, I wanted to harm him. Oh, yes. I wanted to bloody him the way he'd bloodied my mother.

110

My father could barely stand without wobbling. That was to my advantage. Still, he looked stern and threatening with his teeth bared.

"Go ahead, Dad. Come at me. Pretend that you are going to try to grab me by the neck!"

My siblings clustered around my mother. Dad and I now had space. He took one last sip of wine, sucked on his cigarette and put it out in the ashtray on the end table.

Then he lunged at me.

His arms were extended, his hands opened, fingers spread. Perfect. Just the way I'd practiced with Felix on the exhibition team.

Outward chop to his biceps. *Harder! Don't be so timid!*

His arms opened wide. Clear inside chop to his neck. Harder this time.

After the chop, I grabbed his head, thumbs squeezing his temples. Then I raised up my right knee and pulled his head down onto it. Smash. No blood.

Then I pushed him. He hit the hearth and fell to the floor.

There was not a sound in the room, aside from the television. I panted from effort and anxiety, but regained my stance, not knowing what to expect.

Dad stood slowly, shaking his head and rubbing his nose. "Whew," he said and took his seat. Then he laughed, shaking his head as if in disbelief. "You seem to know your stuff. I concede." Then he resumed watching television as though nothing had happened – a classic example of the unpredictable behavior on his part, which threw us off even more.

Although it had probably been obvious on some level before now, my position in the family as number-one-in-charge was suddenly firm.

The next morning, I timed my walk to school to catch Derek. I burned to tell him about the events of the night before, and not just because of the karate. I wanted someone on this Earth, outside of my family, to know the details. But after internal debate, I elected to say nothing, as I wanted him to have the best possible image of me – a desire that was destroyed by his next comment.

"You seem to be gaining weight, girl."

Mortification. But it was true. Mentally I was already planning my new diet when he added, "So you see, my girlfriend is also gaining weight, and everyone thinks it is because she's pregnant. She is not. You believe me, Ann Marie. Right?"

"Of course, Derek. But does it really show?"

"The bab . . . what do you mean?"

"That I have gained weight?"

"Oh, well, yeah it does."

I spent most of my time at school that day thinking about how fast I could get skinny. I decided upon the following diet:

> Breakfast: sugarless rice puffs with skim milk
>
> Lunch: one large apple
>
> Dinner: a small portion of the home meal

But there was a problem with this plan. I had no money to purchase the breakfast and lunch items. After school, I walked to the Safeway store across the street from Kaiser Hospital. I quickly grabbed an empty paper bag from an unoccupied checkout area. I put it into a cart, collected the items for my diet plan, and then walked out without paying.

All the way home, I hid behind trees and bushes, worried that a Safeway employee was following me and I would be arrested.

Only when I finally made it home without incident, did it squarely hit me what I had done. But I did not feel remorse, only agonizing worry that I would still be caught. For years, I had heard my father contriving, lying, and making a big deal out of "getting away with" breaking the rules – a poor example which would become an issue for many of my siblings as they developed into adulthood.   Moreover, after getting away with shoplifting so easily that first time, I began to frequently steal food for my family during those times when our only meal would be the free lunch offered at our respective schools.

One day after school, I stole the ingredients to make spaghetti. That meal was a treat for the kids and me – our usual menu consisted of hamburger patties, boiled potatoes, and a canned vegetable. Nobody ever asked me where all of this food came from, although that particular evening my Dad said, "God damn it, Ann Marie! You know I hate mushrooms, and you just ruined my whole meal." I suspect that my Mama knew what I was doing, though she never said a word, being such a very passive woman.

Treat for dinner or not, the dark of evening always followed. Since the hitting incident, Dad had not been physically abusive toward my mother, though the verbal abuse continued and was upsetting for all of us. I became so afraid that after we kids were in bed, I did not sleep until I was sure that Dad had also gone to sleep. After that horrifying incident when he had hit Mom in the face, I had started sleeping with a knife. I selected the biggest knife in the kitchen drawer, which was about eight inches long. Our knives were dull, and this one could barely cut an apple. But I had made the decision that I would kill him if he tried to harm my mother again. In my mind, this course of action was a clear necessity. We would be rid of him. The consequences did not matter to me.

I had no plans for the summer, but once I learned that Derek would be taking summer school classes at Mount Eden, I talked Pam into enrolling with me. He needed to complete three classes over the summer in order to get his diploma. Of the three, his only elective was a jewelry-making class taught in the shop. Pam agreed to take that class with me if I would enroll in an art class with her. My art skills were not impressive, and I silently groaned at the thought. I agreed so that I could be in a class with Derek, and away from our increasingly hellish home.

It was one evening in mid-July when things finally came to a terrifying climax.

That night, after I heard Dad go to bed, I dared to go to sleep myself. I thought I was dreaming when I heard screaming, but wrenched myself awake and sat up quickly to listen. I heard my mother: "Ann Marie! Ann Marie! Help me!"

I grabbed the knife, jumped down from my bunk, and went out into the hallway.

My four sisters quickly huddled behind, Rosemary clutching my nightgown. "All of you wait right here!" I panted. The door to my parents' room was closed, but I could hear choking sounds.

I threw their door open to find my father in bed, leaning forward, as he strangled my mother. Her eyes were wide. She gasped for air. Rushing to the bed, I held the knife in both hands, raised it over my head, and plunged it into his left side.

Chapter 13:

THE AFTERMATH

The sickening sensation of the steel in my hands piercing my father's flesh caused me such horror that I stopped short after penetrating through his skin. He released my mother's neck, and made a long, guttural sound, groping in the direction of the knife. I dropped the weapon when I heard him grunt, having no idea if I'd really hurt him. He looked at me, eyes wide. I picked the knife up from the bedcovers and held it to his neck.

My mother sat up in bed, taking a long, gasping breath. Worried that my father might strike out at her, I screamed, "Run, Mama!" and stayed put until my mother was safely out of the room.

As it turned out, my drunken father was in no state to retaliate. He clutched his side, moaning, crying, and uttering words that I could not understand.

Still holding the knife, I left my parents' bedroom and quickly looked in the kitchen and living room for my mother. Not finding her, I assumed she had fled from the house.

I ran out the front door, tossing the knife behind the rose bushes that grew over the front window, scratching my hand on the thorns.

I called out, "Mom, where are you?" Although it was near daybreak, my eyes struggled to adjust to the dark as I searched up and down the street, calling for her. Finally, Mom stepped out from behind a bush across the street. She ran to me, shaking violently.

"He could be on his feet, Mom. He's alive. I wish I had killed him, but I didn't. He may come after us," I said, looking back towards our house.

I was so worried about having left my eight brothers and sisters alone in the house with him. Should I go back in? I couldn't imagine how terrified they must be. Should I stay with my mother? Confused and desperate, I decided to run the twelve blocks to Pam Donohue's house. I hoped I could get there without anyone seeing me in pajamas.

The journey seemed to take forever, and when I finally arrived at Pam's house, I tapped – gently, I thought – on her bedroom window. It must have been louder than I intended because suddenly lights came on throughout the house. Pam, along with her sister, brother, and parents, gathered at the front door. Mr. Donohue took one look at me, shivering in my pajamas, and pulled me inside. Breathless and panicked, I managed to say, "I stabbed my father. He was chocking my mother. She looked like she couldn't breathe."

Pam wrapped her arms around me. Mr. Donohue asked where my mother was and if she was okay.

"I don't know, I don't think she was hurt. I told her to run. She's hiding outside the house. I don't know how badly I hurt my dad. I wanted to kill him, get him out of our lives for good. But it made me sick when I felt the knife . . ."

I buried my face into the comfort of Pam's arms. After a pause, Pam's brother Johnny asked, "Do you want me to drive over there and see what is going on, Annie?"

"Oh yes, please, yes! The kids! They must be so afraid."

"Would he try to hurt them, Ann Marie?" asked Mr. Donohue

"I don't think so. He's never hurt any of us. Just my Mom."

"Honey, we need to call the police. God only knows what is going on over there," said Mr. Donohue.

Without waiting for a response from me, he dialed an emergency number, telling the dispatcher to go to Cliffwood. Thank God someone else had taken charge. With that, a feeling of calm came over me.

Of course, my siblings all remember that night. At first, they stayed in their beds, too paralyzed by fear to move. They later told me that the sudden silence after the screams and choking sounds was the worst part.

Eventually, they emerged from their beds. Rosemary remembers Dad staggering down the hallway, where he collapsed. She ran to the bathroom, wet a washcloth, and wiped his brow. Edward remembers Dad moaning and clutching his side, and assumed he was being his usual dramatic self – until he saw blood running down his side. Kathy, having known my plan, later told how disappointed she was to find Dad still alive. They all remember the Hayward Police arriving, along with an ambulance. Only then did my mother come out of hiding and enter the house. She had watched everything unfold from her hiding place across the street.

When daybreak came, I asked Pam if she had any clothing, which might fit me. I just wanted to go to school. Mrs. Donohue was surprised by this, and said that I was surely "in a state of shock." But at this gut-wrenching time in my life, the only thing that kept me sane were the activities that allowed me to escape, where I was able to carry on as a normal teenager. I knew what I needed – a place where life was not filled with constant trauma.

Our first class was the art class Pam had talked me into taking. I was probably the least talented student there, but surprisingly, found that I enjoyed this new means of expression. We had been working on a batik project, and my piece was turning out nicely. However, my feeling of peace was short-lived; ten minutes in, a voice over the intercom said, "Ann Marie McCusker, please come to the office immediately."

To my surprise, two Hayward police officers waited for me outside the door of the art room. Until that moment, it had never occurred to me that I might be in trouble for rescuing my mother – but seeing their stern faces made my heart pound with fear.

"Miss McCusker, let's walk over to the courtyard where we can talk."

I followed them, my stomach churning.

With tiny notebooks poised to record my every word, they told me to describe in detail what had prompted me to assault my father. I felt my eyes widen when I heard the word "assault."

I told my story. The officers nodded frequently. The one who asked the questions seemed very business-like. The other one had a kind gaze and told me that he recognized me from the hospital on the evening, weeks before, when my father had assaulted my mother. Neither made any comment about my story, only asking me where I could be reached after school. I told them I would be babysitting and gave them the address. They thanked me and rose as if to leave.

"Wait, please. Am I in trouble?"

"No, Miss McCusker. You were protecting your mother."

Despite the officers' reassurance, I couldn't shake the feeling that I had done something very, very wrong in the eyes of the law. And yet part of me felt proud for having protected my mother. If I had it to do over again, I would have done the same thing. My only regret was that critical moment of hesitation, because I had failed to kill him. Mission Not Accomplished.

Walking back into the art room, I saw Pam's questioning expression and whispered that I would tell her everything after class. I felt so lucky to have Pam, a loyal and protective friend.

I had no interest in attending the next class, the jewelry class that I shared with my heartthrob. Normally I would have done anything to see Derek, but not that day. Instead, Pam and I walked back to her house, and I was grateful that her parents were not yet home from work. We ate powdered sugar donuts left over from breakfast and drank milk. It felt reassuring to be in a regular home doing a normal activity.

I wanted to know what was going on at Cliffwood, but my family had no phone, and I was too terrified to go back and check for myself. I regretted not having asked the police officers how my Dad was doing. I didn't care about the injury, just wished I knew if he was at home or in the hospital. If he was at home, then that was the last place I wanted to be. If he was not, then I wanted to see my brothers and sisters. It felt as if I had abandoned them.

I had no idea where to turn, and could not calm myself. I did develop a plan. I would go to my babysitting job that night and talk to Judy.

I had been taking care of Judy's two children off and on for two years and had found her to be kind. I would ask to speak with her before she went out with her boyfriend, and share how desperate my home life had become. When she drove me home after her date, maybe she would come into the house with me. Dad would most likely behave if Judy came in the door with me. But after she left . . . that was unknown.

As if reading my thoughts, Pam asked if I wanted to spend the night at her house after my babysitting job.

"Thank you, Pam, yes. Thank you so much!"

"Great. I'll ask if I can use my parents' car and pick you up when you finish. You're done at around nine?"

Judy had a regular childcare provider for her day job, so I mostly looked after her kids when she and her friend, JoAnn, had dates with their boyfriends. Occasionally, JoAnn would pick Judy up at her house with her three children in tow, and I'd watch both sets of kids. I liked that, as I made a dollar an hour, rather than fifty cents. If JoAnn was also there, I would ask if I could talk with both of them for a few minutes before they left. I had no idea what they could do but needed to talk with people whom I trusted. I felt close to these young ladies, and both of them knew a bit about my family circumstances.

Pam dropped me off, promising to return at nine. That evening, both JoAnn and Judy were waiting, their five children playing on the backyard swing set. I had rehearsed my story so much, that by the time I walked in the door, what came out was, "I need to talk with you about my condition . . ." – and suddenly I felt freezing cold, despite the heat of the Bay Area day. I began to shake, feeling chilled to the bone. They sat me down, and I asked for a blanket. Judy brought me an afghan from the couch.

"I mean, no, not my condition, but the condition of my family. I . . . I mean, we . . . we need help." I could not stop shaking. "Can you please turn down the air conditioning? Do you have air conditioning? No, you don't. So why am I so cold?"

This was the first time I experienced that my response to physical or emotional stress was a significant drop in blood pressure, which left me cold and shaking.

"What's going on, Ann Marie?" asked Judy.

"I stabbed my father early this morning because he was trying to choke my mother. He was strangling her. I stabbed him and ran out the door. The police came to school today to question me. I forgot to ask them how bad the stab wound was. I am afraid to go home, but I need to know how my brothers and sisters are."

Judy looked at JoAnn and said, "Let's call the guys, and tell them we'll be late. Better yet, let's ask them to come over and help out here."

"Good idea," JoAnn responded.

Judy picked up the phone and dialed. She spoke in muffled tones, and when she hung up, she said that their boyfriends would be arriving shortly.

The boyfriends arrived within fifteen minutes. Judy suggested that I tell them my story. They listened attentively and asked a couple of questions, mostly about my father's drinking. Then one of them suggested they speak privately among the four of them. I played with the children as the adults went out back on the patio. At one point, I overheard a male voice saying something about not getting involved. About ten minutes later, the boyfriends left.

Judy suggested that the three of us sit at the dining room table and talk this through. Judy's youngest child, a girl about six-years-old, came and sat on my lap. I held her tightly, realizing how much I wanted to hold one of the little ones from home. I smelled her clean hair, wishing that it was Bill, Trish, or Bernadine.

Judy put a meatloaf into the oven which I would have cooked for the children, had the ladies gone on their date. JoAnn took the five kids to a new drive-up restaurant in Hayward called McDonald's. For half an hour, it was just Judy and me. I shared with Judy how many times I had called the police, and how hopeless I felt – as if there was nobody on this earth who could help us. I will never forget her response.

"Honey, the one person on this earth who could change this has refused to do one single thing. You know who I am talking about, don't you?"

I looked down and refused to meet her gaze.

"Ann Marie, look at me. Please. Tell me you know who I am talking about."

I looked away.

Of course, I knew that she referred to my mother. But at that time in my life, I was still unwilling to view Mom as anything other than a victim. It would take one more horrific event before I could fully see her in any other light.

JoAnn returned with the children and three extra orders of French fries for the adults. The kids ate their burgers, fries, and Cokes in front of the television. Judy pulled the meatloaf from the oven, and we grown-ups ate our meal. It became clear that these special women were going to try to help our broken family. Several options were discussed, though Judy eliminated one at the outset: "Do not kill your father!" We all laughed at this, but the truth of her comment was not lost on any of us.

By the time the doorbell rang at nine o'clock, we had a plan. Judy invited Pam inside, eager to share our ideas with her. Someone was going to help. My sense of relief was immense, as was my gratitude for the support.

This is what we shared with Pam.

We needed to get Mama and the children out of the house somehow. The plan was that my sisters Kathy and Rosemary would stay with Judy, in her daughter's room. Since JoAnn had a much larger house, she could provide beds for Mom and the other six kids. I would continue to stay with Pam. "Is that okay?" I asked Pam. She nodded yes. Additionally, JoAnn had a friend who knew a social worker, whom she would call Monday morning. The problem with all of this was that my Dad worked strictly on commission at some fly-by-night used car lot on Mission Blvd. He was there whenever it suited him. Could JoAnn and Judy go to the house with the assurance that my father would not be home?

The next day was a Saturday – typically a good day for the used car business, so I was relatively confident that Dad would go to work at some point in the afternoon. Judy suggested that in the morning, she would call the car lot and fake a story about how she had seen a car that interested her. She would say that she had picked up one of my father's business cards earlier in the week and specifically ask to speak with him. That way, we would get information on his whereabouts and condition.

The ladies insisted that I go back to Pam's house for the night, and they would call me when my family was safe in their respective care. Despite the fact that I hadn't done any babysitting that evening, they each gave me five bucks. Pam and I got into her parents' car and I asked her to cruise slowly by our house on Cliffwood Avenue. She reluctantly agreed.

I could see nothing through the closed drapes as we drove up. I asked Pam to park around the block and wait for me. Pam thought this was a very bad idea, and let me know. But I was determined, so Pam agreed – but insisted on coming with me.

I wanted to know if my father was at home. And I needed to know if the rest of my family was safe.

We crept toward the house, hiding behind the palm tree in the front yard. The drapes on the front window made it impossible to see much, but a few drapery hooks were missing, leaving a gap that might be possible to peer through if I could just get close enough. I moved muscle by muscle, as Pam kept watch from behind the palm tree.

The gap turned out to be just what I needed. To the left, I could see as well as hear the television. No sign of my siblings, but by eleven o'clock at night, they must have been in bed. To the right, I saw Dad in his chair. He had a glass of beer, and cigarette smoke curled into the air. I strained to look further to the right and managed to make out the figure of my mother. I turned to Pam and gave her a thumbs-up sign. Then without a further word or gesture to Pam, I walked through the gate that led to the backyard. My parents usually left the back door open, and I hoped to get to the kids' bedrooms to check on them.

Once in the backyard, I stopped and opened the side door to the garage so I could duck in for a moment and steady my nerves. The familiar stench hit me immediately. For months now, we'd had no garbage service, so the garage was packed with paper bags full of debris. Fearing I would gag, I quickly closed that door and walked toward the back door, which led to the bedrooms.

As I did, I felt my hair pulled back harshly, raising my chin high. A hand firmly covered my mouth.

My mind raced. It couldn't be my father. I had just seen him in the living room. I could have easily released myself from this simple hold; my arms and elbows were free, and my karate training nearly kicked in. But before it did I heard Pam whisper in my ear, her voice firm: "Are you out of mind? Let's get the heck outa here, right now!"

I pushed her hands away and gave her a scornful look, which I doubt she saw in the dark. "Knock it off, Pam!" I whispered back. "I need to check on my brothers and sisters." But I knew that Pam was right. What would I have done if one of the kids had awakened to find me standing there? I realized I wasn't thinking clearly and needed to just go home with Pam. I reminded myself that a reasonable plan was in place for the next day, and I needed to follow Pam's advice.

The following day, our plan worked flawlessly.

By that afternoon, Rosemary (8 years old) and Kathy (14) had gone to Judy's, and everyone else was safely settled at JoAnn's. Rosemary missed not being with Mama, so my benefactor-ladies kindly made a switch; Rosemary and Billy (7) swapped places. Everyone was safe and happy.

My Dad arrived home from work that day to an empty house. No note had been left. His wife and children were simply gone. I was delighted that he finally had consequences to face as the result of his actions – but at the same time, annoyed with myself when I realized that part of me felt sad for him.

Dad called at Pam's house that evening. The Donohues told him that they had not seen me. To be safe, I took to entering and exiting the house through the side door off of the garage, and only after someone took a look to see if the coast was clear. He knew where Judy lived because for the past two years he had occasionally driven me to her house to babysit. That worried me. When I mentioned this to Judy, she instructed the kids to keep the door locked, and only leave the house to go into the backyard.

For the next two weeks, Kathy was to become the official daytime babysitter for Judy's kids. The timing was perfect, as the regular sitter wanted to go on vacation with her family, and Kathy was delighted to earn some money.

The following week would prove a very eventful one for the McCusker family.

As for myself – knowing that I was no longer alone in trying to fix my family was a profound relief. All I wanted to do on Monday morning was to go back to summer school as usual. Naturally, the thought of seeing Derek was a huge incentive.

In our jewelry class, which was held in the shop, Derek asked if he could speak with me privately on our break. I watched the clock, waiting for that moment, fantasizing that he was going to ask me out. By this time, it was common knowledge that his girlfriend, Shirley, was indeed pregnant. His being with her was just a mistake, I rationalized . . . maybe he actually could be attracted to a 'good girl' like me? Then reality gripped me; I realized that, most likely, Derek would finally tell me the truth about Shirley's condition, and that would be it.

At break time, we walked across the quad at Mt. Eden, and Derek settled himself on a set of steps. I had applied my grape-scented lipstick and flashed my best smile, as I took a seat on another step. "Got something to tell you, Annie!"

He had a habit of swiping his right index finger over the tip of his nose when he had something important to say. Everything he did enchanted me, so naturally, I found this gesture endearing. "Well, tell me," I asked, appearing as nonchalant as I could.

"I joined the United States Marine Corps a few weeks ago. Passed all of the stuff, and I leave for boot camp next month."

I have little memory of my response, other than babbling something about how he could be killed in Viet Nam. I do recall how devastated I felt, and the emptiness in my gut. My fantasies had been destroyed.

When Pam and I arrived at her home after school, Mrs. Donohue was already back from work. She answered the phone when it rang. It was my father.

"No, she is not here. You what? Sold all of the furniture? Emptied out the whole house? Why would you do that to your poor family?"

I realized that she was repeating everything that he said, for my benefit.

"You did it because they obviously do not want to live with you? You sound like you've been drinking, Mr. McCusker. You need to get some help before you lose your family forever. Maybe they do hate you now, but you could change that if . . ."

I made eye contact with Mrs. Donohue and held out my hand. I wanted to talk to him. Rage consumed me, and when I took that phone I proclaimed to him for the first time: "I do hate you. I hate your guts!"

His voice changed. It sounded evil. In my mind's eye, I could see his eyes become slits. Maybe he was even clenching his fists. He hissed, "Oh, and I hate you more than . . ."

Mrs. Donohue took the phone back.

I was shaking, but not crying.

"I wish I had killed you!" I screamed toward the phone, and then ran to Pam's room.

It was 3 P.M.; I wanted to call JoAnn and Judy and tell them what had happened, but they would not have been home from work. I could have spoken to Mom at JoAnn's, but I did not want to talk with her.

Two hours later, the phone rang again. Mrs. Donohue quickly picked up, and handed the phone to me, saying that it was Kathy.

"Hi, sis. How are you?"

"Are you okay?" What's going on?" I asked.

"Everything is great! I love it here. I figure I earned eight dollars today and Judy said she would pay me more if I do some housework."

Kathy also told me that Judy's son had just bought the new Rolling Stones album. Even Billy likes it, she said. I listened and said nothing about my exchange with our father. Then I heard Mrs. Donohue calling everyone to dinner.

"Gotta go, sis. Time for dinner. Did you talk to Mom today?"

"No. You?"

"Nope. I'll call her tomorrow."

We said goodbye.

Every few weeks, Mrs. Donohue would serve a breakfast for dinner. On this night, we were having waffles. I asked to put peanut butter on mine and Mrs. Donohue obliged. I loved watching the peanut butter melt into each tiny square. Then I piled on the jelly. For a second I worried about my weight, and then remembered that Derek was leaving anyway, so I ate with relish. Plus, given how upset I was by the conversation that I'd had with my father, this dinner was oh so comforting.

How naïve I had been to think that we could pull off our plan without him reacting strongly. But I was determined to fight him with every resource at my disposal. I took a big bite of waffle, savoring the melted peanut butter.

I was still a kid. What did I know?

Chapter 14:

OUR VOICES ARE HEARD

I awoke early after a fitful night's sleep and decided to get up. The house was quiet, so I tiptoed past the bedrooms to the living room. I sat in Mr. Donohue's reclining chair and picked up the magazine he'd left there. When I reached to toss it into his magazine rack, I noticed pictures of young men on the cover, wearing various service uniforms. It was a *Time* magazine, featuring the faces of the fallen. This reminder of the escalating Viet Nam war naturally diverted my thoughts to Derek. I read the cover story. It sounded as if most of the casualties were Army and Marine Corps soldiers. I'd paid little attention to this war, despite its strong presence in the news every night. Still, I knew that Viet Nam was a dangerous place to be, and now, it felt personal.

Derek would soon be off to Camp Pendleton, and then Viet Nam. I considered telling him about the *Time* article but didn't want to jinx or worry him. Instead, I would share how proud I was of him. And in that way that the young feel so invincible, I simply couldn't believe that *he* would ever be a casualty.

Was I really a low-class girl pretending to be someone else? In hindsight, I'd felt that way ever since I was little. What guy could possibly be interested in a girl whose family was such a mess?

I realized that I would have only four more days of structured contact with Derek before summer school ended. He could have any girl that he wanted, and yet he seemed to like *me*. So maybe there *was* something special about me.

Pam had set my hair for me the night before, and I longed to get the rollers off. When I heard footsteps approach the family room, I rose to greet Pam. But it was Mr. and Mrs. Donohue, who left for work at 6 A.M.

"Little Annie Roonie! Why are you up so early?" said Mr. Donohue.

"Ann Marie, go back to bed," said Mrs. Donohue in a snarly voice. "It's too early for you to be up. You need your sleep." She plugged in the percolator and gave me a look that suggested I might be invading their time.

"Okay, see you this evening. Thank you again for having me here. I really appreciate it, Mr. and Mrs. Donohue."

Rather than going back to Pam's room, I retreated to the other side of the house and into the bathroom. I carefully removed the pink netting that held the rollers in place overnight. Then I took out the pins and rollers and put them in the roller drawer. I shook my head, enjoying the clean bouncy feeling of my hair, which would soon be teased and stiff with hairspray. I turned to see Pam waiting to use the bathroom.

"Mornin', Annie. You're up early."

"Yep, I'll get outa here so you can go."

"Thanks."

Pam was generous with her clothing, yet my options were limited to what she had that fit me. Pam was taller than me and thinner. (It would be another year before Mount Eden High allowed girls to wear slacks to school, so I squeezed myself into her skirts.) Pam's continuous kindness did so much to sustain me during those troubled times.

Our six-week summer school session would finish up on Friday, and today was Tuesday, July 29. Being away from my family gave me a brief respite from obsessive worry about them. I needed a few good nights' sleep. While there was a part of me that wanted nothing more to do with my crazy family, during idle moments the heartache returned, and it was difficult to distract myself. My siblings were suffering. Fear defined their existence.

Squeezing into Pam's skirt, I put on one of her large peasant blouses. I carefully applied make-up, trying to cover the zits that always seemed to pop out overnight, and checked my appearance in the mirror. Sometimes I thought I looked cute, and occasionally, even pretty. I was told that I had a "good personality," but that just didn't cut it when your figure lacked curves.

In jewelry class, everyone scrambled to get projects finished before the end of the term on Friday. Though I tried hard throughout class, I did not manage to be alone with Derek. Walking with Pam back to her house, I said little and tried to ignore the empty feeling that churned in my gut. If I dwelled on it, it became fear.

Talking helped, so I said to Pam, "I know this is dumb, but with all of the stuff going on with my family, the one thing that I looked forward to was being able to talk to Derek. That didn't happen today."

"Yeah, we were all busy finishing up our projects. But I did notice Derek looking at you a couple of times."

"No way."

"Yes, way. I mean it! You looked so cute today, Annie!"

I instantly felt better.

After dinner, gloom settled into my thoughts. I had no idea what would become of my family. We couldn't live with friends forever, and now there was no furniture in the house. In desperation, I considered quitting school and getting a job, so I could take care of the family. But I could never make enough money to support ten of us. Plus, I liked school. I feared the thought of going home and wished I could live with the Donohue family forever.

I called Mom that night. I hesitated to ask if she knew about Dad selling everything from the house on Cliffwood, so I chose to not bring it up unless she did. She didn't mention it. She did tell me that JoAnn and Judy had set up an appointment with a social worker, who might be able to help. "They needed to get the same few hours off, and next week was the first time they could manage that," my mother said.

This was good news, and I appreciated the effort, which had gone into it. JoAnn and Judy were single mothers with custody of their children, and both worked full time, so it had taken some planning on their part to arrange this meeting.

"Just stay where you are, Mom, okay? Who knows what help might be out there? We've never shared our home life with anyone, but it's time, Mom."

"Okay, honey. How are you?"

"I like the peacefulness, Mama," I said.

I remember little else about this conversation with my Mom, though I do remember asking to speak with the little ones. I had been eleven years old when Trish was born, twelve when Bernadine had come along and felt as though I had raised them. One took the phone from Mom, as I waited for the other to pick up the extension in JoAnn's bedroom. They both cried and told me they wanted to go home. I was puzzled. Surely, they must be so much more comfortable at JoAnn's house, free from trauma and unpredictability?

"Soon, my babies, soon," I reassured them. But this was a lie. I had no idea what the coming week would hold for any of us.

On a brighter note, during my phone conversation with Kathy, she told me that she and Billy loved it at Judy's and hoped they could stay there forever. It was so easy for me to understand that. None of us brought up my father. I imagine that we all wished that he would simply disappear and leave us alone.

Then it was Wednesday, and I had only three more days to make any connection with Derek. After that, it would only be a matter of time before he received his orders to report to boot camp. Not wanting to rely solely on the jewelry class, I came up with a plan. I had a friend who was on our high school newspaper staff. I would ask her if I could interview Derek about his reflections on going to Viet Nam, so I could submit it to the school newspaper in the fall. It worked like a charm. Derek was more than willing to meet with me after school, while I interviewed him.

My last question was, "Are you afraid you will be killed?"

"Well, of course. All I can say is that I will leave that decision to God and my rifle." Then he laughed and tousled my hair, which was so stiff with Aqua Net that it barely moved. I was not pleased with that gesture, which seemed like the sort of thing I would do to one of my little brothers or sisters. Was that how he thought of me? I felt unattractive and walked back to Pam's house feeling dejected.

I thought about checking in with my family but decided against it. "Tomorrow," I thought. I wanted one more day of pretending that I actually lived at Pam's, free of the turmoil of my family . . . and a bit of time to lick my wounds as it began to hit home that Derek was not attracted to me. I felt more acutely than ever that, while I might have a good personality, I was not sexy, and I spent the rest of the evening wishing I was thinner, or didn't have acne, or had nice clothes, or that Derek had gently touched my face instead of messing with my helmet hair. I would call the family tomorrow, on July 31st. It would be Mama's thirty-sixth birthday.

And what a birthday that turned out to be . . .

The next day, Pam and I arrived home from school to a ringing phone. We agreed that I would not answer, just in case it was my father. When Pam picked up, I heard her say, "Try to calm down, Kathy! I can't understand a word you're saying." I gestured toward Pam with my hand open and she gave me the phone.

"Annie, Dad knows where Mom is! Should I call the police?"

"Where are you?"

"Judy's."

"Where's Judy?"

"Her kids tried to call her and left a message. She's on her way home now. Dad showed up here, Ann Marie. He took Billy and me back to Cliffwood." Her voice broke as if she could barely get words out. "It was really horrible. Then he dropped us off back here."

"Where's Dad now?"

"Don't know. But he has JoAnn's phone number."

"What about JoAnn's address?"

"*I* don't know her address, Ann Marie!" she screamed into the phone.

"Are you and Billy okay? Did he hurt you?"

"Not really."

"Tell me what happened!"

"He came through Judy's backyard and got into the house. He told Billy and me to get into the car, and then he grabbed Billy by the neck. Oh my God, oh my God, poor Billy! Then he dragged Bill out of the house, and I followed them and got into the car. Billy wet his pants, Ann Marie. He was so scared. He wet his pants!"

Despite her hysteria and my own, not to mention Billy's audible sobs in the background, details began to fall into place. Kathy went on to describe how our drunk father had taken them back to the house on Cliffwood. The place had been almost empty of furniture, but full of clutter. One chair remained in the living room . . . the one Dad always sat on. On the floor next to it lay a rope and a knife.

My mind flashed to the word "knife." I wondered if it was the same one I had wielded.

Dad had proceeded to tie Kathy up, threaten her with the knife, and demand that she say where our mother was. Kathy refused.

Billy was seven-years-old. As Kathy tells it, Billy grabbed Dad's arm and said, "Please Daddy. Let Kathy go. Mom is at JoAnn's house and we don't know where that is. We just have the phone number. Please let Kathy go. Please, Daddy!"

Only then did our dad fall to the floor in tears, clutching his head. "Oh my God, oh God forgive me! What have I done, what have I done! Oh God, forgive me, children!" And with that, he returned my brother and sister to Judy's house, with JoAnn's phone number in his pocket.

By this time, my father had called my mother at JoAnn's, demanding a meeting with her, telling her nothing about the terrifying act he had committed toward two of their children. She agreed, told the kids what she was going to do, and left, assuring them that she would be back soon.

By the time she arrived back at the house, JoAnn was home. My brother, Tom, remembers how concerned JoAnn was about the possible outcomes of this meeting between my parents. She told Mom how Dad had terrorized Billy and Kathy just that afternoon, having learned what happened from Judy.

"Are you crazy?" JoAnn challenged my mother.

Mom told JoAnn that she would talk about it after the children were asleep, glancing toward Tom, who pretended to be reading a comic book but had been listening intently.

Having heard this, Tom seemed to assume my usual role, as the eldest on the scene. Once all the children were in bed, he crept downstairs to a spot where he could overhear the grown-ups' conversation. To his utter amazement, he heard Mom tell JoAnn, "I am leaving in the morning with my children and we are going home."

Tom made himself visible at that point, saying, "I don't want to go home, Mom."

"It will be alright, son. Now, go back upstairs and go to bed . . . *now.*"

Unknown to Tom or my mother, JoAnn proceeded to make some emergency phone calls.

Maybe the Hayward police were concerned that my father would grab more of his children and terrorize them, or that my mother would actually take her children 'home' to that empty house on Cliffwood. Maybe they finally realized that this man could be a danger to his own children.

In any event, the police acted, although they thought it wise to wait until the McCusker children were fast asleep in bed. But they apparently failed to consider that being awoken in the middle of the night and bodily put into a police car could be a damaging memory for a child. Or maybe the police forgot to explain to my frightened siblings that they were there to help them. Or maybe they did, but children of that age simply lacked the capacity to understand. I do know that in the spite of the trauma their actions put my siblings through, Hayward P.D.'s intent was honorable that night, and I for one felt grateful that our voices had finally been heard.

Two patrol cars arrived at JoAnn's to pick up Tom, Ed, Jim, Rosemary, Trish, and Bernadine. One went to Judy's to fetch Kathy and Billy. The other one went to the Donohue house to get me.

Tom, Ed, Jim, Rosemary, Patricia, and Bernadine were taken away in their pajamas. The boys rode in one car, the girls in another. Later, they would tell me that they were terrified because they had no idea what was happening. They distinctly remember our mother crying, trying to reassure them that "everything will be okay," as she watched her children placed into the squad cars.

When the police car arrived at Judy's house, she pleaded with the officers to allow Kathy and Billy to stay with her. Kathy remembers how Judy told the officers about the kids' traumatic day and assured them she would take good care of them, and to please just allow them a restful night's sleep. "But they are not safe here at all. Look what happened this very afternoon," was the reply.

I was most fortunate. Being sixteen years old, the officers informed me that I could either stay with the Donohue's or go with them. But before I could make that decision, I needed to know where everyone was being taken.

"Snedigar Cottage," one of the officers told me. "It is in San Leandro. A place where kids of all ages can stay while the court figures out what's best for them. It's a good facility. They will be safe, well cared for, and all together."

"I should go," I said, though the terrifying uncertainty made me want to stay with the Donohue family.

Then the doorbell rang. A sickening chill washed over me, and I involuntarily rose to my feet, moving to stand behind one of the officers. "My Dad. It might be my Dad," I said, in a shaky voice.

"Probably the social worker," one of the policemen reassured me.

He was right. Mr. Donohue answered the door and showed a nicely dressed woman of about thirty into the family room.

She looked over at the two officers and said, "Got here as soon as I could. I needed to get the other children settled in at the Cottage." She went on to introduce herself to the Donohues and me, as Mrs. Etrium let the police officers know that they could leave, if they wished. Before departing, each one of the Hayward police officers came over to me and shook my hand. One smiled and wished me luck.

Over the next half an hour, the social worker outlined what was going on.

The McCusker children, for their own protection, were now temporary wards of the state of California. She would be in contact with my mother first thing in the morning and request an interview with her. She also needed to interview me and a couple of the older children. She guessed that a court date would be set sometime in the next few weeks to determine our future custody. There was a kindness about Mrs. Etrium's tone that made me trust and like her. She was young, attractive, and looked fresh, despite the late hour.

She asked me a lot of questions, and her expressive eyes softened as she listened to my replies. At one point, she stood up from her seat and came over to sit next to me on the couch. Ever so gently, she put her hand on my knee and said, "You kids have been through a lot. I am so sorry."

Mrs. Etrium encouraged me to spend the night "right where you are." She told me that she could pick me up at 8:30 in the morning. I could see my brothers and sisters, and then she would need to talk with me at length.

I noticed Pam nudge her mother, at which point Mrs. Donohue said, "We will be sure she gets there in the morning, Mrs. Etrium."

After Mrs. Etrium left, Pam and I went to our room. Though I was exhausted, I doubted that I would get a wink of sleep. It was already Thursday, early in the morning.

Thursday!? Oh my God, my mother's birthday! Not only had I forgotten, but also I realized that I'd hardly given my mother a thought all day. I assumed that she was still at JoAnn's – but then JoAnn had called the police after Mom agreed to meet with my father. Maybe JoAnn had been so furious with her for that, that she had kicked her out? No, surely JoAnn realized, as I did, that this could turn out to be Mom's chance to get rid of my Dad for good.

Since it was too late to call JoAnn, I put my head on the pillow – and quite surprisingly, fell into a deep sleep.

Chapter 15:

THE COTTAGE

It was difficult to contain my eagerness to see my siblings – and my anxiety. I was short-tempered with Pam when she missed a turn on our way.

The Cottage turned out to look nothing like its name suggested. The location was lovely with trees, blooming flowers in neat beds, and footpaths throughout the grounds. But in place of the quaint little structure I had pictured were modern, well-kept, institutional-looking buildings. A central administrative hall was flanked by two large wings. Behind them, other buildings nestled into the foothills. In the distance, I could make out a play yard and basketball court. A large sign read, "Snedigar Cottage, State of California, and County of Alameda."

I ran through the entrance doors as Pam parked the car. I found myself in a large sitting area, with chairs of various sizes, and pillows on the floor. Behind a glass window sat a woman on the phone that looked up at me and smiled as I entered. To the left of the sitting area stretched a long hallway, brightly lit by large windows on both sides.

I identified myself to the receptionist, saying that I had an appointment with Mrs. Etruim, but hoped to see my brothers and sisters first. She picked up the phone, turned away from me, and spoke for a few minutes to someone. The scent of patchouli she exuded was strong enough to make me sneeze as I waited. Putting down the phone, she spoke into a microphone, and I could hear her voice boom through speakers: "All McCusker children please report to the lobby. Attention staff, please have all McCusker children report to the lobby."

From the large windows, I watched them come in groups down

the hallway. The little ones, Trish and Bernadine, came first, a staff member holding their hands. She unlocked a door and let them run to me. They clutched me and began to cry. I sat on the floor and they climbed onto my lap. Was I there to take them home, they asked? My eyes filled with tears, but before I could answer, I saw Billy walking down the corridor alone. The receptionist opened the door for him. Tears streamed from his huge blue eyes. He wiped his nose on his shirtsleeve and sat behind me, his arms wrapped around my neck.

I gasped, feeling literal pain, as if someone had stabbed me with a long sword. Paralysis threatened to overcome me. I could not breathe. The little ones were terrified, unable to understand that they were at the Cottage for their own protection – and I had played a major part in bringing this upon them. *Hey Lord. It's me, Ann Marie. Help me.* My mother had taught me to pray such words in moments of desperation.

Realizing that I was close to crying, I put my head down and willed myself to recover. I managed to put a courageous smile on my face, just as I saw Kathy and Rosemary come running down the corridor. Smiles blossomed on their faces when they saw me. We hugged and kissed, and before I knew it, Tom, Ed, and Jim were also there. It remains the most powerful moment of my life.

The older kids understood this catastrophic change in their lives on some level, but the little ones could not comprehend this and were simply bewildered. I tried both comforting and explaining, hoping to help them understand they were safe here, and that this was only temporary. The four older ones seemed to get what I told them, but the four younger ones could only repeat how much they wanted to go home, which left me feeling raw, diminished, and powerless.

"Don't any of you worry. I will get a job and rent a house, and we will all be together," I told them, honestly believing every word in that moment.

I hadn't noticed Mrs. Etrium's arrival in the lobby. She moved toward us with kind hesitation.

"Your parents will be here in a few minutes, children. All of you can stay right here until they arrive, and I am going to take Ann Marie to my office so we can talk."

My siblings were clearly excited by the news that they would soon see Mom and Dad. I was considerably less than thrilled; I had not expected their visit to coincide with mine and had no desire to see either of them. Pam and I walked down the corridor with Mrs. Etrium, and as I turned to look back at my siblings, I saw my parents walk in. As I had been earlier, they were quickly surrounded by loving children.

My interview with Mrs. Etrium lasted for two hours. Our session was taped and a stenographer took notes. I told them everything. Mrs. Etrium shook her head several times and finally said, "I think we have enough here to hold these children and get a court date, which will most likely be in about three weeks. Ann Marie, I'll need to interview your brothers and sisters, as well as your parents. You can visit your siblings any time."

Pam had sat quietly with me during all of this, and now said, "Annie, we can probably use my brother's car, or parents'."

I smiled at her in thanks but had an urgent question at that point. "So, Mrs. Etrium – if you decide they can't go home, and . . ."

"I do not decide anything," she interrupted. "There will be a judge who decides."

"Okay," I said, "but if the *judge* decides they can't go home, what will happen to them? Well, I guess to me, too?"

"Then we will be looking at foster homes, Ann Marie. Which may be a far better way to go than what you have all been living through."

"All of us would still be together?"

There was no mistaking the doubt on her face. "That's a lot of children to place with one family, Ann Marie. But I would do my best to make that happen."

"They – that is we – would hate being separated. In fact, I think

141

that would be terrible, Mrs. Etrium. People have a hard time understanding how close we all are. We . . . ah, we . . . we've been through a lot together." It was frustrating; it felt as if there were no words I could use to adequately explain how important it was to all of us kids that we stuck together, for now, and forever. "Isn't there any other option?" I asked.

"That part could be up to your mother. If she leaves your father, maybe the state would allow the children to go home with her, provided he is not around. But I am just guessing, Ann Marie. These decisions are up to the judge, not me. But I can guarantee you one thing. These children will not leave here until a judge evaluates your family situation."

During the subsequent week, I visited my brothers and sisters as often as Pam could drive me to the Cottage. I made it five times, always worried about bumping into Mom and Dad. Gratefully, that never happened. After six days, Mrs. Etrium called me at the Donohue home. She said that Kathy hated life at the Cottage, and was threatening to run away. She asked, "Do you think she would really do this?"

"Yes, absolutely she would."

Kathy was a rebel; she had become used to a very free lifestyle, which required being away from her crazy family as much as possible. While my response to the family turmoil had been to get more involved with school, Kathy's outlet was to hang out with the tough crowd.

Bless Mrs. Etrium. After our conversation, she convinced the Donohue family to allow Kathy to stay at their home with me until after the court date. During the next few weeks, I felt closer to Kathy than I had in a long time. We sought one another out, seeking comfort and relief from despair. We slept in the same twin bed and held one another tight. Tired and bruised, we wrapped ourselves together into a cocoon.

Kathy drove Mrs. Donohue crazy with her willy teased hair, excessive make-up, short skirts, and messy habits. I began to quietly tidy up after her.

During her first night with us, Kathy told me that our father had been coaching the children to lie about what went on in our home on Cliffwood. She quoted him as saying, "If you tell the truth, you will be placed into foster homes, separated for the rest of your lives, and probably never see one another again!" Up to that point, I had avoided asking my siblings about our parents, perhaps taking too literally Mrs. Etrium's mandate to have no contact. But in that moment, I could not help myself from further quizzing my sister.

"So, Mom and Dad always came to visit you together?"

"Yep."

"So they are back together?"

"Yep."

"And did Mom say anything when Dad told you guys to lie?"

"Nope."

And for the first time in my life, I stopped seeing Mom as the victim.

God help me, I was ready to square off with my mother in this battle, as wrenching as that felt, if that's what it took.

As upset as I was by Kathy's comments, I was also concerned by her reports about how my siblings fared at the Cottage. They had been separated by gender and age. Trish and Bernadine shared a room. So did Tom and Ed shared a room, with Jim right next door. But Rosemary and Bill, being younger, were in a different wing of dormitories, each bunked with a stranger, and had little interaction with their siblings. I wished that they would have put all of the children together, or at least nearer to one another. We were all accustomed to being crammed together in a three-bedroom house. We were close, both physically and emotionally, and during the rough times, it was a comfort to have that proximity.

It was Billy who suffered the most. One day during a break from "school" (it was summer, but the Cottage residents had structured instruction) Tom, Ed, and Jim went out into the courtyard to play pick-up basketball. Unknown to them, Billy watched from across the fence. He gripped that fence, watching his brothers play, as tears streamed down his face. Tom remembers being the one who finally spotted Billy, and all three older boys walked over to him. They knelt to his level and tried to comfort him, but he was inconsolable. I die a bit every time my mind wanders to this mournful story, knowing now what fate was eventually to befall my brother Bill.

Cottage policy was to administer castor oil to the children each evening. They detested this. Other than being separated, that eventually became their only complaint. Ed actually liked living there. Food was abundant. The children were provided with more clothing than they ever had in their lives. And they slept peacefully, no longer awakened by shouts, screams, or fears. Ed told Mrs. Etrium that he would rather stay at the Cottage than go home.

I felt guilty for not being with my siblings, unable to shake the feeling that I had abandoned them, and envied Kathy for her first-hand knowledge of how they fared.

At last, Mrs. Etrium informed me that the court date was set for August 18, 1967, and that my parents had requested a court-appointed attorney. The prospect of dealing with an attorney in court frightened me. I imagined being grilled to pieces like I'd seen television attorneys do on Perry Mason. There were to be three witnesses for the State: me, Judy, and JoAnn. Mrs. Etrium hoped to avoid having any of the other children testify, though Kathy would likely be called into the court. I was instructed, quite adamantly, to have no contact with my parents or their attorney.

The days seemed to drag on, until finally, we had our day in court.

Chapter 16:

OUR DAY IN COURT

The custody proceedings were not to be held in a courthouse. For the comfort of children, the Cottage had its own accommodations for hearings involving its juvenile residents. I was relieved that we would not visit the Alameda County Courthouse, which had always looked cold and foreboding to me.

Mrs. Etrium had taken Kathy and I clothes shopping a few days before. We had previously owned nothing appropriate to wear in court. On the big day, Kathy wore a ruffled white blouse with black trim and a below-the-knee black skirt. I thought she wore too much make-up, but at least her hair did not resemble a rat's nest. I was proud that my sister looked so nice – not in the least bit like a hood. It was important to me that we both looked suitable, not like a couple of ragamuffins.

Kathy and I arrived at the Cottage early so we could check in with Mrs. Etrium. Her office door was open. She smiled and asked us to come in and sit down. We both confessed to feeling nervous about the day's events, but Mrs. Etrium did her best to reassure us by helping us understand what we could expect.

"Ann Marie, Kathy, you two will testify first. Your parents will not be in the room, so you can tell the truth without worry. I will ask the questions, though the state district attorney could ask you to elaborate or ask questions of his own. After you leave, your parents will be brought in to testify. The district attorney will question your parents. They have an attorney who will also be speaking."

"That's it? First us, then Mom and Dad?" asked Kathy.

"My hope is that the judge will also want to speak to Judy and JoAnn. Then your brothers and sisters might be called in, as well. I hope not. Not only have they been through enough, but they are adamant about wanting to go home, especially since I told them about the possibility of going into foster care."

"Well, I can tell you, Mrs. Etrium – *I* would rather go home than live with strangers!" Kathy said. "At least then I'd be able to stay over with some of my friends."

"I understand that, honey. But what if you could go home without your father being there? There is a strong possibility that will be the outcome."

"But how would we get by, I mean, who would pay the bills?" I asked.

"The state of California would . . ." Mrs. Etrium's words were interrupted by a buzzing noise that seemed to come from her phone, so loud and unexpected that Kathy and I both jumped. "It's time to go," said Mrs. Etrium, "but first your brothers and sisters would like to see you. They are waiting in the antechamber."

Given the potential outcomes of the process I had set in motion, I could not help but wonder if I had done the right thing. That uncertainty chipped away at my confidence. I was sixteen, so legally I never had to live with my family again, and it would be my choice. But my siblings?

Two moments from that day are permanently burned into my memory. The first is my initial sight of my siblings.

The antechamber, as Mrs. Etrium had called it, was a narrow room with wooden furniture and no windows. My siblings were seated on a long bench in order of age: Tom, Ed, Jim, Rosemary, Billy, Patricia, and Bernadine.

The first thing that struck me was their appearance. They looked

146

scrubbed and coiffured, neat and tidy, solemn, wide-eyed, dressed in new clothes and new shoes, and their hands folded on their laps. None of them greeted me with their usual enthusiasm. Instead, they looked at me in a stunned and fearful way. This tableau still haunts me. I wanted to scoop them all up and take them away.

Were they all feeling as deserted and abandoned as I was? It had been a long time since I had felt safe and protected. All those times I had called the police and nothing to show for it . . . it had felt like a nightmare . . . and now that the help I had longed for had arrived, I was simply not sure that I was ready for the responsibility which went along with it.

Ed broke the spell, asking, "What are you going to say, Ann Marie?"

I squeezed myself onto the bench between the little ones and took their hands. Trish and Bernadine barely stirred, as though too much movement might mess up their crisp dresses and pretty hair. "Just the truth," I said.

"Do you think I will have to tell them about what Dad did to Kathy?" Billy asked.

"Mrs. Etruim hopes that none of you will have to speak, or even go into the room."

"Then why are we sitting here all dressed up?" Tom asked, challenge in his voice.

Kathy told him, "Just in case, I guess. But Mrs. Etrium told Ann Marie and me that if Dad stays away, maybe we can all go home."

At that moment, Trish broke ranks and ran for the closed door. "I want to go home! I want Mommy and I want to go home." Kathy caught Trish, knelt down, and hugged her. Then Mrs. Etrium entered the room and told Kathy and me that it was time.

Kathy and I were showed to chairs just outside of the hearing room door. Kathy elbowed me and pointed down the corridor. There

147

stood our mother and father, looking anxious and forlorn. Mom had lost weight and wore one of my old shift-style dresses. She stood still, watching our father, who paced and smoked a cigarette.

Then she turned and saw us. We made eye contact for a few seconds, and she dropped her head. That was the second sight I will never forget. I loved Mom so much and wanted to run to her, but it felt as if there was a wall between us. Kathy did stand and start toward Mom, but I grabbed her arm and pulled her back into her seat. She did not resist, and slumped down, sighing loudly.

"It's like we're enemies. I just hate it, Annie. I hate this so much."

"Yeah, me too."

A part of me wanted to call the whole thing off. Another part urged me to press on but feared that Kathy would cave in, and not tell the truth. I looked up and down the hallway for Judy and JoAnn. No sign of them.

For ten excruciating minutes, Kathy and I sat there, mere yards from our father and mother, yet unable to acknowledge them. Even without Mrs. Etrium's edict that we have no contact with them prior to the hearing, it would have been emotionally impossible to engage them at that moment, as much as our hearts might have wanted that. As the minutes dragged on, Dad popped out an adjacent door a time or two with his cigarettes, and I could see that he pointedly avoided making eye contact with me and Kathy.

At last, a door opened from the hearing room and out walked Judy and JoAnn. They'd been the first to testify, and I was eager to learn how it went, but before I could ask, I heard my name called.

As hard as I try to recollect my testimony on that day, I always draw a blank. All I can remember is a judge, and two tables near him. At one table, a man sat next to Mrs. Etrium, and at the other, a man sat alone. This second man wore a nice suit and didn't move much.

At some point, a break was called. Kathy and I were instructed to wait in the antechamber. My siblings were no longer there. We paced until Kathy said that she needed to get outside and find a cigarette she could bum. While I was normally a Nazi about her smoking habit, in this instance, I couldn't have cared less.

We walked out to a patio. A man was out there smoking, and I recognized him as the guy who sat at the other table in the courtroom. Kathy asked him for a cigarette. He handed her one and lit it for her.

"Are you my parents' lawyer?" I asked.

As he drew himself up a bit, I noted he was a tall man, with a large belly that hung over his belt. He moved his tie to the side and put his cigarette pack and matches back into his shirt pocket. His suit jacket covered the pack. He glanced at me, tipping his head down so he could look at me over his glasses. His face had no expression.

"Yes, so I can't talk to you." He dropped his unfinished cigarette to the ground and stepped on it. Then he turned toward the door.

"Do you understand how terrible that it has been for us kids?" I blurted out.

"Kids are resilient," he said. And off he went.

I felt diminished by his words. *Resilient?* After all of the horror that we'd experienced, somehow all of us kids should be flexible enough to simply shake it all off? All of the anger that I had been holding in my heart boiled to the surface. I felt my face flush with heat, which traveled down to my hands. They reddened and began to shake. I felt intense hatred toward this man and poisoned with rage. Fully and completely, I now wanted to win. I wanted society's acknowledgment that there had been profound suffering in my family.

After what felt like an eternity, most of it spent waiting in the dreary antechamber, the judge rendered his decision. Mrs. Etrium met with all nine of us McCusker kids. She summarized the terms.

We were to live with Mom. Dad had to live elsewhere.

Dad was to have no contact with the family for six weeks, during which time he was required to have psychiatric treatments twice a week.   After that, depending upon the recommendation of his therapist, he could receive some visitation rights to see the family. We were informed that my father had managed to refurnish the house on Cliffwood. He had also rented a small studio apartment for himself. I have no idea how he had pulled all of that off financially, but clearly, he had received help from somewhere.

All nine children were to return to Cliffwood in two days, after a home inspection by the state. A van would pick up Kathy and me at the Donohue's at one o'clock in the afternoon, then return to Snedigar and bring the other seven home at two o'clock.

On the day that Kathy and I were to leave, Mrs. Donohue served our favorite breakfast. I wondered when I would ever have waffles again. Before leaving the table, I thanked the Donohue family for the countless times they had helped us. So did Kathy. Then my sister and I went to the bedroom and packed our belongings. We each filled four paper bags.

"Let's walk over and see Mom," Kathy suggested. "We can get back in time to get a ride on the van with our stuff."

I liked this idea, imagining my mother at home all alone. We told Pam what we were doing, and assured her we would be back before lunch. As my sister and I began walking, we wordlessly took the long way home, toward Palma Ceia Park.

"You think there'll be any food in the house?" asked Kathy.

"I sure hope so. I have no idea what to expect. I just want to see the kids."

We arrived home and I knocked on the door. Mom answered. The look on her face may have mirrored my own. Tenderness. Hurt. Uncertainty.

"Why the heck are you two knocking on the door at your own

house?" she smiled.

Kathy and I hugged Mom. For a long time.

"Youse girls hungry? I can make you some lunch now, or we can wait until the rest of the kids get here. Maybe a snack?"

Kathy and I each opened a cupboard in the kitchen. Leaving them open, we moved to the next, then the next, until all of the food cupboards stood open. Amazingly, Mom had stocked all our favorite cereals: Coco Puffs, Sugar Pops, and Frosted Flakes. Even the cookie cupboard held dozens of bags of cookies. Lunchmeat, cheese, milk, and ice cream filled the refrigerator. The place was fully stocked! Mom smiled proudly as she watched Kathy and me pull out cereal bowls, then fill them with Coco Puffs and milk.

After this treat, Kathy and I returned to the Donohues to pick up our paltry belongings, and the official van arrived to take us home. About forty-five minutes later, the van brought my other seven siblings to the house on Cliffwood.

All ten of us sat in the living room, speaking little at first. My brothers and sisters seemed hesitant, cautious . . . the silence between us felt eerie and unnatural.

Finally, Edward said, "Dad's not here, right?" Oddly, he addressed this question to me, rather than to our mother. When I answered in the affirmative, little Trish asked me, "And he's not coming back tonight?"

At this point, Mom chimed in, explaining that our Dad was not allowed to come home until he got well. Then Jim said that he was hungry, and it was as if a dam burst. All seven of my youngest siblings piled into the kitchen and indulged in the wealth of sugary cereal, as Kathy and I had done about an hour before.

Without Dad around, the house was an easy and peaceful place to be. The little ones, Patricia and Bernadine, began sleeping with Mom in her bed. That allowed Rosemary to stretch out in the twin bed she usually shared with Patricia. The boy's room smelled better because they had all stopped wetting the bed. I sat in Dad's chair at night, making room for however many could fit with me. We still had no television or phone, so we sang. We laughed. Mom played with the little ones. Then we would all sleep soundly.

There were a few flies in the ointment of our otherwise renewed lives. Some of the neighbor kids had been forbidden to play with the McCusker children. I recall Rosemary walking into the house in tears on her second day home from the Cottage. She had knocked on a friend's front door, and the mother had answered. Rosemary did not remember the exact words spoken, but the message was not lost on her. The neighbor girl was no longer allowed to play with her. I comforted my young sister as best I knew how.

A stigma had arisen around the McCusker family, and the kids paid the price, even though it was not their fault. But looking back, I guess that we were "resilient" for the time being . . . until much later, when our personal issues began to surface. At that moment, though, we were a step or two above surviving. And that was progress.

Chapter 17:

TURNING POINT

For a month and a half, life took on a calm rhythm. We slept and ate our meals on schedule, and walked about the house without fear.

That summer was a hot one, and on the inauspicious day, which ended our family reverie, I watched the younger children run through the sprinkler out front, laughing with glee. The little ones ran up to me after their romp, and I wrapped towels around their small, chilled bodies. The day was beautiful. Tranquil. And then I looked down the street.

My father was walking toward us. *Oh God, no!*

I felt my pulse in my throat. Quickly clutching Trish and Bernadine, I told them to go into the house, as I stood out there like the Praetorian Guard. I even folded my arms across my chest.

"You are not supposed to be here," I said.

"Ah, c'mon Ann Marie. I just came by to see if the kids wanted to swim in the pool at my apartment. That's all. It is so damned hot."

I couldn't help but notice how healthy he looked. No redness on his face. An easy, confident gait. He hadn't looked so good in years.

Before I could answer, the front door opened and out poured Billy, Trish, and Bernadine. They ran into their father's waiting arms, as he knelt down to gather them in for hugs. My mother followed right behind them.

"Mom," I said at the top of my voice, staring at my father, "I'm going to the neighbor's house to ask if I can use the phone. I am going to call the police."

My words were lost as the kids snuggled into their father's arms. My mother didn't answer.

And was Mom smiling at him?

He squeezed past me, went into the house, and soon afterward left with the three youngest, taking them swimming. *Did I imagine it, or was my mother actually glad to see him?*

I found myself gripping my mother's arm as I directed her to one of the dining rooms chairs. Sitting next to her, I was surprised by the gentleness in her enormous blue eyes. I felt myself relax, wanting to fold myself into her arms. But with effort, I remained stiff as I spoke to her, keeping my gaze on the table.

"What are you doing, Mom?"

"Ann Marie, just look at him. Can't you see he has changed? Believe me, losing you children shook him to the bone. It was horrible for him, and he knows he was responsible. Can't we agree to give him one last chance? Please, honey."

I do not remember what I said, but I must have caved in. I went outside, experiencing again the creepy sensation I'd often had in my father's presence. Technically, he was still mandated by the court to stay away. He was to have *completed* intensive therapy, after which he could *request* visitation.

Naturally, my father paid no attention to any rules. It wasn't long before he had moved back into our home.

In those days, little was known about alcoholism, and treatment tailored to it was nearly nonexistent. My father was being treated for a stress disorder. He had several prescription bottles on his end table. He particularly complained about the medication called Thorazine, as it made him sleep all the time. What a blessing *that* was!

After just a few days, he flushed every one of his pills down the toilet. Shortly thereafter, he announced that our family would be moving.

We hastily relocated to a house on Coronado Street. I never did get a straight answer from my parents about the circumstances surrounding this move, but soon figured out for myself that it was an evasive tactic on my father's part to avoid supervision from the State of California. We had no phone and gave no forwarding address. Fortunately for us kids, Coronado was only a short walk away from our former home on Cliffwood, so at least we all remained in the same schools.

But had no one in authority thought to check our schools? My brother Tom recollects this time as when "the State of California really dropped the ball." They allowed us to disappear. Again.

For three months, my father behaved himself.

Then, around Thanksgiving of my junior year at Mount Eden, I walked in the door from school and there he sat in his underwear, with a beer and a cigarette. I recognized the flushed look on his face, the dullness in his gaze. "Hi honey," he said. "And how was school today?"

I said nothing. I walked to the bedroom I shared with my four sisters, stopping by the kitchen to grab a grocery bag. I filled it with make-up, pajamas, and a change of clothing. As I left the room, I noticed Mom standing in the hallway.

"What are you doing?" she asked.

"No, Mom, the question is, what are *you* doing? Are you going to do anything about Dad? Will you call Mrs. Etrium?"

"I can't call her. They will take the kids, and you know it!"

"You had a chance to change all of that, Mom, and you didn't! You just let him back in here like nothing ever happened." I had raised my voice, catching the attention of the little ones and Dad, who were all the living room. Trish and Bernadine just looked on silently, with round eyes. Dad got up and staggered into the hallway.

"What the hell is going on here?" he slurred.

"Absolutely NOTHING, Dad," I said, "except that I am leaving."

I pushed past my Dad, opened the front door, and left. My mother came to the door and shouted, "Get your ass back in this house!" *She never cusses*, I thought vaguely, through the haze of anger filling my brain.

I did not turn back to look at her. And it would be many more years before I ever slept under the same roof as my father. I thought about my brothers and sisters. Who would be there to comfort them? To sing to them? To hold them during storms? I was shrouded with remorse and yet determined.

Determined to do what? At that moment, I am not sure I could have articulated it. But many years later, I came across a poem – 'The Journey' by Mary Oliver – which captures in an uncannily perfect way what I felt on that bleak evening in Hayward, California:

THE JOURNEY
By Mary Oliver

One day you finally knew
what you had to do, and began,
though the voices around you
kept shouting
their bad advice--
though the whole house
began to tremble
and you felt the old tug
at your ankles.
"Mend my life!"
each voice cried.
But you didn't stop.
You knew what you had to do,
though the wind pried
with its stiff fingers
at the very foundations--
though their melancholy
was terrible.
It was already late
enough, and a wild night,
and the road full of fallen
branches and stones.
But little by little,
as you left their voices behind,
the stars began to burn
through the sheets of clouds,
and there was a new voice,
which you slowly
recognized as your own,
that kept you company
as you strode deeper and deeper
into the world,
determined to do
the only thing you could do--
determined to save
the only life you could save.

(Reprinted with Permission)

Chapter 18:

HOMELESS

I started walking with no destination in mind. I had no idea I would be leaving home, so I lacked any plan.

Despite this, I walked briskly and with confidence, even finding myself smiling as I recalled the plan my friend Shari and I had formed in junior high for times of trouble: get the bus to Southland Mall, go to Sears, hide in one of the tents on display, and wait until the store closed. We never actually did this, but we each still checked the camping section whenever we went to the mall, just to be sure that a good-looking tent was available.

But if not Sears, where to go? Naturally, the Donohue family came to mind. They had been more than kind but had also gently let me know after taking me in the last time that they had done all they could.

My smile faded quickly. If I followed through with this, I would have no place to go. Sitting on a curb a few blocks from 'home,' I considered my options.

Should I call Mrs. Etrium? I struggled with this possibility. Contacting her would get the state of California involved again. *I will not be the cause of more trauma for my brothers and sisters. I just need a place to stay, that's all.*

Besides Pam, there were two other friends who were part of our close-knit group at Mount Eden: Gail and Terri. Gail's parents were strict and neither friendly nor welcoming, so I decided to call Terri. I always carried a few dimes with me (never knew when I might need a pay phone in the middle of the night), and found a phone booth. No answer. My dime was returned, and I started walking in the direction of Terri's home.

Dusk was falling when I knocked on the door. Mrs. Cook answered. Terri was out and not expected home for another half hour, so I told Mrs. Cook an abbreviated version of my story. She listened wordlessly, gave me a hug, and assured me that I could stay for a few days until I "got things straightened out."

The furnishings in the Cook house were more Spartan than I'd realized. I did know that Mr. Cook suffered from some illness and couldn't work. On top of that, it looked as if they were poor, too. A cot was set up for me in the girls' bedroom, placed between the twin beds Terri and her older sister slept in. It wasn't much, yet I was grateful.

Each morning, Mrs. Cook gave her five children a small allotment of money. I learned about this the first morning at breakfast, when Mrs. Cook quite nonchalantly included me, giving me bus fare to get to school. Now prepared, beginning the second day, I made myself absent. I began packing a small lunch, and Terri shared her money to pay for the bus.

My friend Gail and I shared a P.E. class together. As we dressed down for volleyball, Gail asked me how it was going with Terri's family.

"Her folks are really nice, but I am so uncomfortable because I have nothing! Not only do I eat their food, but I use all their other stuff, too. Shampoo, toothpaste . . . I need a job so I can give them money or buy my own stuff. But where would I keep it? And Mrs. Cook mentioned about staying just a few days. I sure don't want to, but if things got really desperate, I guess I could go back home . . ."

As Gail and I continued our conversation, I became aware that one girl there in the locker room was listening and looking at me. When I looked back, her eyes avoided mine. *Guess it could be much worse for me. I could be her . . . whatever her name is.*

The girl was just pulling the required white-and-blue-striped gym shirt over her head. As she did, her wig tilted slightly back. She quickly adjusted it.

Gail and I had privately discussed her during the months we shared in the tight proximity of the locker room. The wig was so obvious, but *the girl* had no eyelashes or any body hair anywhere. Her eyebrows were penciled in, quite thickly. *The girl* was teased relentlessly by some of our meaner classmates. And not a soul ever spoke to her, including me. If we happened to make eye contact, I would offer a weak half-smile. A few times I muttered a terse "Hi," as we crowded with other girls through the only set of doors to the locker room. When it came to *the girl*, I felt like such a coward.

After the gym, Gail and I returned to the locker room and hastily changed for our next class. To my astonishment, *the girl* crossed the bench to my side of the row and spoke to me.

"You need a job? I wasn't spying or anything, Ann Marie, but I heard you tell Gail you need a job."

Whoa, she knows our names!

"Well, I sure do. Why do you ask?" I wanted to ask her name, too, but didn't – I felt too embarrassed.

"I have a babysitting job after school, three days a week. I have to give it up because I have to be away for a few months."

She filled me in on the job details: Young married couple with two children, eighteen months and four years old. The mom worked three days a week, as a nurse at Kaiser. The dad was a social worker and took graduate classes at night. Fifty cents an hour from four until ten at night. Dinner all prepped, just need to cook it. Babysitter eats with the kids.

"I gave my notice, but really need to leave as soon as I can. I can talk to Mrs. Taylor this afternoon, and maybe you can meet me at their house the day after tomorrow."

161

"You are kidding me! This is unreal, uh . . ."

"Jocelyn. My name is Jocelyn."

I saw Jocelyn in P.E. class the next day and let me know that arrangements had been made with the Taylors. She handed me a folded sheet of loose-leaf paper with an address written on it. This entire thing felt like a miracle.

My new job began the following Monday. Having helped with babies since I was very young, I was a natural caregiver for Jennifer and Travis. Before long, this kind couple caught on to my living conditions, particularly since I could only offer the Donohue's phone number instead of my own. Once they understood the situation, I had a place to stay overnight three days a week.

I never saw Jocelyn again after that Friday when she hooked me up with the Taylors. Mrs. Taylor told me that Jocelyn had cancer, and was being treated at Stanford Medical School in Palo Alto. Her prognosis was highly doubtful. She preferred to be called Josie. I still wish that I'd taken the time and effort to find these things out myself.

So, for a while, I spent my nights in a sleeping bag on the floor of little Jennifer's room, or at Terri's, or sometimes at the Donohue's. My family lived only one block from Mount Eden, so occasionally, I would pop into the house and grab something to eat, and always when I was certain that Dad was not there. It was such a comfort to see my siblings. We'd play and laugh, and always before I left, Mom and I would have a cup of tea. Mom never once brought up the topic of my absence from the house.

Derek wrote to me at my 'home' address. Mom would tuck letters for me into her purse and pass them along during a visit. I could see that she enjoyed bestowing such a precious gift to her daughter. We read his letters together. Unfortunately, there was nothing romantic for me to censor.

In one particular letter, Derek wrote that he would be home for the holidays and wanted to see me! He had completed USMC boot camp, plus some additional training, and would be off to Viet Nam after his leave. I wondered how I would manage to hook up with him, given my transient life.

Of course, I knew where Derek's family lived, so when the holidays drew near, I began walking past his house as though I was headed to the Safeway a few blocks away. For six days, I maintained this mobile vigil, walking past his house with feigned purpose, crossing the street to Toppers, a youth hangout, and beginning the circuit over again. And then, one day, there he was, standing outside of Toppers. I spotted him and I froze.

Derek looked lean and smart in his uniform. His thick brown hair had been shaved short.

Our long hug wasn't long enough for me. I felt such comfort in that embrace. My breaths became long and deep, and I experienced the soulful state that we'd learned to access in karate.

At first, our conversation was disappointingly inane. How's it going? How long ya been home? Seen so-and-so yet?

Then, finally: "Well, you look great, girl! Wanna get a Coke and some fries at Toppers?"

Seated together at a table in Toppers, Derek and I talked about Boot Camp, and his being singled out to walk point in a platoon. He had a good eye and had been trained as a sharpshooter. He was very proud of this, boasting that he would be "out there first," leading his fellow soldiers.

After a while, describing his new life in the military, which clearly excited him a lot, Derek asked me how I was doing.

My letters to him, while he was gone, had been upbeat, if slight. I would try to be witty, and being a flop at that (or so I felt), struggle to find topics. Our common interest in karate was not enough. Once, after he'd told me about receiving some recognition for superior marksmanship, I'd sent him a gigantic cigar as a congratulatory joke.

Unfortunately, his drill Sergeant had made him smoke it.

I had told Derek little about my family life in those letters.   But as we sipped our Cokes and munched on fries there in Toppers, I found myself sharing far more than I'd intended.   More than once, I caught myself rocking back and forth – a subtle behavior, which cropped up when I felt uncertain of myself.

Derek waited for me to lift my head, as I had been staring down at the empty red plastic basket that had held the French fries.   His eyes softened.   I could see that he didn't judge me.

"Wow, Annie.   I'm so sorry.   Stay strong, okay?   You've got a head on your shoulders.   Promise you'll write and keep me posted about all this stuff, okay?"

"I will, yes, of course, I will.   Thank you, Derek," I said.

We walked slowly back to his house.   Then it was time to say goodbye.   He removed his cover and kissed me.   Then we parted ways.

Wow.   *Was that a kiss?   Like a real kiss?   Well, maybe it wasn't exactly a romantic one.   Right?   It didn't seem passionate or urgent, coming from a guy heading to Viet Nam.   But it wasn't exactly the way you'd kiss your sister . . .*

In a spin about the kiss, I found myself headed toward my family's home.   I was in a fantastic mood.   It felt like a good day to pay a visit.

Walking up the path to their front door, I noted the unkempt front yard.   Nothing unusual there – ours was always the worst on the block.   There was no car out front, so I assumed that my father was not at home.

Inside, it was empty, and eerily quiet.   I walked through the living room to the dining area, where household items lay strewn all over the place.   Clothing littered the hallway leading toward the bedrooms.   I still hadn't heard a sound, and shouted, "Hey, where is everybody? What's going on?"

Looking into the girls' room, I noticed the absence of Herman the Mouse and Kelly the Rabbit from the little ones' shared bed.   Patricia and Bernadine never went anywhere without their stuffed animals.

That's when it hit me. They were gone. I was alone in my life.

My body felt hollow, as though my insides were suddenly gone. Vacant, empty, and without substance: this house, and me.

I went back to the living room and sat on the floor as dusk passed to darkness. I must have dozed off, but awoke completely alert and knowing exactly where I was. *Might as well sleep here until the landlord comes to get rid of the furniture.*

I wrote to Derek that night using the forsaken end table and lamp. In a drawer with the playing cards, I'd found a small pad of paper with Edward's handwriting – scribbles scoring a game of rummy. I could tell it was Ed's writing because he was a southpaw, and smeared the ink just like Dad.

Writing to a friend brought me comfort, and helped me explain myself to myself. Postage was free when writing to anyone in or bound for Viet Nam, so there was no need for a stamp. I walked out to the corner mailbox and dropped the letter inside.

I slept in my old bed, went to school the next morning, and did my babysitting job.

Derek's response was quick, written the morning he shipped out to Viet Nam.

"I have an idea!" he said in his letter. "What if I wrote to my family about letting you stay at our house until you graduate? My bedroom is empty."

He went on to describe the three folks in his household whom I had never met.

"My sister, Jessica, is three years older than me and a junior at Cal State Hayward, majoring in education. She is very straight and conservative, a serious student, and not at all like me. Dad works two jobs. He carries mail during the day and works processing film at night, twelve-hour days. He is a good guy, but my mother runs the place. She is a drill sergeant and not so easy to get along with. I needed to get out of there so I joined the Marine Corps. That's a story for another day, Annie."

It sounded like an uncomfortable situation, but I wasn't about to rule it out. Previously, I had imagined that if my semi-nomadic life became desperate, I could always move back in with my family. Now I didn't even have my own address anymore. But I was blessed with good friends, and that night I was scheduled to sleep at the Donohues. It would be good to talk to Pam.

Pam had likely badgered her family to allow me to live there on a more regular basis, so had I never brought up the topic, yet secretly hoped that they might extend an invitation. It didn't help my cause, though, that they viewed their three-bedroom home (master bedroom for the parents, one bedroom for Pam's brother, one for her and her sister) as crowded, and dreamed of having a bigger house one day. Their place seemed palatial to me.

That afternoon on the way to the Donohues' house from Mount Eden, Pam and I chatted as usual, while I tried to think of a way to approach the topic of a more permanent home for Ann Marie McCusker. About a block short of the house, she stopped and said to me, "Before we get to my house, I need to talk to you about something."

Man, she looked so serious, and I felt a stab of uncertainty in my gut as I said, "Okay."

"I went over to the Riccis' this morning during third period. I know I should have talked to you about . . ."

"Oh my God, how embarrassing. Oh my God, Pam. They must think I am such a loser.

Who did you talk to? His mom? I hope they at least got a letter from Derek about this! For gosh sakes Pam, I know you were only trying to help, but . . ."

. . . but, it had already been decided for me, by two well-meaning households. I was about to move in with a family I had never even met, with little to offer them in the way of financial reimbursement.

Later that evening, I rang the Riccis' doorbell just as I managed to drop a pile of my belongings into an adjacent bush. Jessica opened the door, saw what had happened, and chuckled as she helped me retrieve the contents of my toppled paper bag. I liked her immediately. We exchanged quick introductions, and she said, "Come in and meet my mother."

Mrs. Ricci sat on the couch watching television. As I walked in, I noticed immediately that the house was impeccably clean and tidy, the floral-patterned sofa and matching chair covered in protective plastic. Mrs. Ricci went to the television, turned it off, and gave me a stiff hug. "Let me show you Derek's, I mean, your room," she said.

I followed her down the hall, Jessica carrying one of the three paper bags, which held my worldly goods.

I will never forget my first impression of that room. A small twin bed rested up against one wall, flanked by a dresser. Across from the bed was a large table, adorned with a statue of the Blessed Virgin at least two feet tall. On each side of the statue sat a picture of Derek, both of them in uniform. Dozens of votive candles, all lit, sat in front of the statue and pictures. It was an altar of sorts. I felt as though I had walked into a church and found myself whispering as I put my bags on the bed.

During the months that I stayed there, the candles were replaced and lit each day. It comforted me to fall asleep to the soft lights flickering throughout the night, illuminating Mary's compassionate face. I never felt alone in that room.

Chapter 19:

MY JUNIOR YEAR

By the second half of my junior year, life at school was suddenly amazing. People treated me differently. My peers stopped referring to me exclusively as a brain and/or 'nice girl,' but also as personable, funny, and a good listener. More relaxed, and getting more regular sleep, I began to thrive in the social arena.

Without the stress of living with my family, a whole new world opened up to me. Based on my GPA, I was inducted into the California State Scholarship Federation. I joined the drama club and got a small part in a production of "Inherit the Wind." I was elected to a student body office and selected as 'queen' for a Hayward city fundraiser, which came with a gala formal dinner. For once, I didn't worry for one minute about having a date to escort me.

My self-confidence blossoming, I auditioned for the annual musical at Mount Eden High School – to this day a much-anticipated event in the East Bay area and a big moneymaker for the school.

That year, the Mount Eden performing arts department put on the musical "Guys and Dolls." The library allowed students to check out an album overnight, as auditions involved singing at least one song from the score. I went into my tryout with little knowledge of the female leads, though I felt inspired by the role of Adelaide. An alto like me, her character was wonderful: Jersey/New York accent, full of life, and the opportunity to dance. With my whole heart and soul, I wanted that role.

I didn't get the part.

Mrs. Eaton, the drama teacher, had a certain senior in mind for that role, and it became obvious from the callbacks that she would be cast. But she asked me to continue practicing the songs of the soprano romantic lead, Sara Brown. I stretched my voice to its thinnest, uppermost octave, somehow managing to make it carry over the orchestra and choir. As a result of my hard work, I was indeed cast as Sara Brown!

It was late April, and our first performance was to be on May 16th, three days after my seventeenth birthday. Playing Sara successfully was going to take a lot of work, so I walked to school from the Riccis each morning singing my heart out. *"I'll know when my love comes along . . ."* On the way, I often passed a man who was out watering plants. And while it was my intention to pause vocal practice when I passed him, he heard me anyway; one morning he shouted, "You're getting better every day! Just remember to breathe from your diaphragm and you'll be fine." I replied, "Thank you, sir!"

In the ensuing weeks, rehearsals routinely lasted well past dinnertime, and Mrs. Ricci was kind enough to always put a meal in the oven for me. I learned to recognize which plate was mine, as she also put one in the oven for Mr. Ricci, whom I always beat home. I couldn't babysit after school with this schedule, so my friend Pam took over for me. She even loaned me the paycheck that she received for this, so I would have some money. I assured her that I would pay her back, as I had recently learned that I would have a job over the summer.

My high school counselor had submitted my name for a newly funded federal program called Neighborhood Youth Corps (NYC). At the time, I knew no details, only that I would be working full-time at the Naval Air Station in Alameda for one dollar and sixty-five cents an hour. With such a formidable amount, I hoped to pay Pam back *and* give the Ricci family some room and board money. The thought of finally having some substantial money was heavenly. It was demeaning to constantly feel like a pauper, and I enjoyed the prospect of being able to financially hold my own.

At one rehearsal in early May, with only ten days until opening night, Mrs. Eaton felt that we were all doing so well that she allowed us to leave at the unprecedented time of five-thirty. I returned home to the Ricci residence, finished my pasta dinner, and sat down in the living room to join Mrs. Ricci and Jessica as they watched television. The Ricci family watched the six o'clock news every evening, and in those days it was always dominated by Viet Nam. Mrs. Ricci was glued to the television, saying nothing but an occasional, "That Johnson bastard!"

She and Jessica sat together facing the television on the plastic-covered couch. I sat in the living room's one uncovered chair, in which I could actually feel the fabric.

Suddenly, in the corner of my eye, I noticed a Marine in dress blues with a piece of paper in his hand, walking toward the house. He looked at the house, then down again at the paper, as if checking the address.

My heart stopped. I gasped. Jessica and Mrs. Ricci looked at me. They couldn't see out the window from their vantage point.

Finally, the Marine walked off in the opposite direction. With an immense inward sigh of relief, I smiled at Derek's sister and mother. We all resumed watching the news.

And then, the doorbell rang.

I rose to answer the door. There was the Marine.

"May I speak with Mrs. Ricci?"

She rose to her feet. The Marine stood squarely in the doorway, a solemn look on his face. In a split second, my joyful life had become a nightmare. *Please, God, please*, I prayed silently.

Mrs. Ricci became hysterical. "NO!!!" she cried. Jessica put her arms around her.

Should I be here now? What do I do?

Words were exchanged with the Marine. In shock, I had no idea

171

what was said. I snapped to attention when Jessica spoke my name.

"Ann Marie! Call my father. Right now.   Tell him to come home."

Me? I have to call Mr. Ricci? Oh, please. Not me.

"Jessica, what should I say?"

"For God's sake, just make the call, Ann Marie. Just tell him to come home!"

Go to the kitchen and pick up the phone. I dial and ask for Mr. Ricci, please. I tell them it is an emergency. Mr. Ricci comes on the other line.

"Mr. Ricci. This is Ann Marie. Jessica asked me to call you. You need to come home right now, sir. *Right now*, okay?"

I heard the alarm in his voice as he directly, *so* damned directly, asked, "Is it Derek?"

I don't want to tell him that his son is dead. I don't want to be the one.

"Please just come home, Mr. Ricci."

Unable to prolong that awful conversation, I hung up.

Mrs. Ricci was screaming. I re-entered the living room to the sight of her pounding on the Marine's chest. I felt sorry for him, having to deliver such life-ravaging news to people who could not possibly have been prepared to receive it, all the while bound by duty to maintain his stoic Marine poise.

After what seemed like an eternity, Mr. Ricci finally arrived home.

I felt like an outsider in this moment of family tragedy. Without a word, I left, going to the only place I really could: Pam's house and the Donohue family.

Later, around ten o'clock, I returned to the Ricci home. The house was dark and quiet. I crept inside and was startled to find Mr. Ricci sitting in the living room. His eyes were swollen.

He said quietly, "He died yesterday, May 5. We requested his body be shipped to New York. Our family is there, and that's where he'll be buried. We want you to come to the service. He cared about you, Ann Marie. I know you have the musical, but we will pay your way if you are able to go."

I had no idea what to say. My own grief, bad as it was, must have been orders of magnitude less than theirs. I finally managed, "Anything I can do now?"

"No. My wife is heavily sedated and sleeping. You might want to check in on Jessica, though her door is closed. I don't know what she needs right now. Her room is dark. The doctor gave her a pill."

I walked into my room – that is, Derek's room. It was dark. No candles flickered around the room's shrine.

I can't sleep in this room. Where to go? If Mr. Ricci was not in the living room . . . Standing uncertainly in the doorway, I felt a gentle touch on my shoulder. It was Derek's sister. "I just don't want to be alone tonight. Do you want to sleep in my room?"

"Yes, I do, Jessica. Thank you."

Her room, like Derek's, had a twin bed. She pulled off the blankets and pillow, left the room for a moment, and returned with more bedding, making a bed for us on the floor.

We talked through the night. Sometimes we cried, but mostly we had no idea what we were supposed to be feeling. Some moments we felt nothing. We may have even laughed once or twice. Maybe we were in shock. We both knew we didn't want to be alone.

Next morning, I went to school as usual. How strange it felt. Shouldn't there have been something very different about the world?

I arrived early enough to visit Mrs. Eaton's classroom and speak to her about attending Derek's funeral. I was not thinking clearly and imagined that I could just miss one performance, because the memorial service was to be a Roman Catholic Mass on in New York on May 19th, a Sunday. That was the day of a two o'clock matinee.

Mrs. Eaton was uncharacteristically sweet and tender with me at first, her eyes weepy. But then, with visible effort, she became her firm teacher-self and told me that I could not go, reminding me that we didn't have understudies. "If you're not there, Ann Marie, just as is true for any of the leads, the show does *not* go on."

I left her office saddened, but there was something else, which I recognized after a moment of reflection as a sense of self-importance. And with that came a sense of shame.

The first thing I did when the Riccis left for New York was to pull the plastic covering off of the furniture. Derek had complained about the stuff and I told myself that I did it in homage to him. I sprawled the length of the couch, careful not to let my shoes touch the fabric.

I had less than an hour before needing to return to Mount Eden. It was opening night, and I could not reconcile my opposing feelings: elated and excited, yet profoundly sad. How was that possible?

I'd stopped by my family's house, wondering if the owner had cleared things out yet. The furniture was still there, and clothing was strewn everywhere. It was an eerie feeling, to realize that they were gone.

Mrs. Eaton had given each of the four lead actors complimentary tickets for opening night, and I wanted someone from my family to see me perform. Despite my ambiguous feelings toward my father, I realized I wanted him there. His love of singing and his theatrical nature had rubbed off on me. Dad would have been proud.

But I told myself that I didn't give a damn. The complimentary tickets would be kept as memorabilia in a scrapbook, forever.

After weeks of hard work perfecting my performance, weeks anticipating my joy on-stage and the approval of friends and family, it suddenly felt wrong to be excited. I was alone and in a house of grief. My family had disappeared. One of my best friends was dead. Shouldn't I be feeling depressed?

Too nervous to eat, I walked to Mount Eden early, hoping that I could get started on my make-up. Maybe the drama classroom would be open, the girl in charge of readying the actors already there.

Thankfully, she was there, and I was able to distract myself with preparations. The doors to the theatre stood open, and I heard the full orchestra practicing the overture. The "Guys and Dolls" refrain soared across the quad. I stared at my image in the mirror and realized I was smiling. *I am ready. I am elated. Grief and joy can coexist for me.*

For two and a half hours, I was Sarah Brown. There was one particular high note early on which worried me, but I hit it effortlessly. After that, I simply had fun. I nailed my solo, "Ask Me How Do I Feel," a piece which allowed me to sing entirely in my most natural range.

On the day after the opening-night performance, the theater critic for the Hayward *Daily Review* commented that "this young actress sure knows how to belt out a song," – and as hard as it was for me to fully believe, those words were about me. Such unaccustomed and public praise had me floating on cloud nine for parts of the day, like my character singing with glee while tipsy from too many drinks in Cuba. But in the next moment, I would feel a darkness enter my spirit, and barely manage to hold my head up in the halls of Mount Eden.

My classmates seemed equally conflicted. Some congratulated me on my musical success, while others were grimly sympathetic about Derek. But clearly, being in the musical had moved me up a few notches on the social ladder at Mount Eden. When my peers playfully greeted me in the hall with, "Good morning, doll!" or "How's our best doll this afternoon?" I beamed inside.

Such recognition meant the world to me, but it could not sustain me when I returned to the empty Ricci home. I challenged the eerie vibe there one evening by lighting every candle on the dark altar that paid homage to Derek. I said one Our Father and three Hail Marys. Ritual had always comforted me, and at the time, that kind of Catholic recitation was the only manner of praying that I knew. I had no sense of a personal God from whom I could seek comfort using my own words. And so I just cried, alone and by myself, my pain the sum of losing Derek, plus the reality that my family had taken off without a word.

The Riccis were due home late in the day on Tuesday, May 21st. Before they arrived, I checked the mail and found a letter from my mother, postmarked Tucson, Arizona.

Her letter began with an apology for leaving without telling me, which she said had been at my father's insistence. He knew full well that his children were still wards of the state of California, and that he would not have been permitted to leave the state with them. He had also worried that it would only be a matter of time before I called Mrs. Etrium about his continuing bad behavior and drinking. I understood my mother's explanation, though I seethed with anger at my father for yet again disrupting the lives of my siblings so that he could continue his miserable lifestyle at their expense. And my spineless mother – how could *she* do this to them!

Mom's letter went on to say that they were renting a trailer in a mobile home park. It was a three-bedroom with no air conditioning, but at least the park had a pool. There had been no sense enrolling the kids in school, she told me, with only a few weeks left in the school year. They didn't have a phone yet, but as soon as my dad got work, they would get one and she would call. And would I please try to not be upset with her . . .

I held the letter in my hands, rocking back and forth and back and forth on Derek's bed, suppressing the urge to scream. I was lucky enough to have broken free from this madness, but my brothers and sisters were still captives. As they got older, I hoped that they would be able to escape, too.

In the meantime, what could I do to help them? At first, I could not think of one single thing. But then I realized that as soon as I had my summer job, I could write a letter to each and every one of my siblings, and put a dollar in each envelope. They would be overjoyed and could go to the store and buy candy, or a Coke and fries. Yes, that is what I would do! That would be a huge treat for them. Satisfied with this plan, I folded my mother's letter and put it on top of my schoolbooks.

I decided to wait until the next day before writing a response. Glancing at the clock in my (Derek's) bedroom, I realized that the Ricci family would soon be home. I'd already made sure that the house was spotless, especially fussing with the plastic furniture coverings to make sure that it all looked properly back in place.

I was gazing out the living room's picture window when I noticed their car pull up. How should I greet them? None of the words that came to mind felt right, so I decided to busy myself by dashing out to the car to help with their luggage. As I approached the car, Mr. Ricci opened the passenger door then walked toward me carrying a small bundle wrapped in his jacket. Before Mrs. Ricci or Jessica had time to leave the car, he handed me the bundle and quietly told me, "Quickly, put this under the bed in Derek's room."

I did as I was told and was heading back toward the front door when the family walked in.

Still clueless about what to say, what fell out of my mouth was "*Welcome home.*"

Mrs. Ricci burst into tears. Normally neither an affectionate nor demonstrative woman, she hugged me and held on tight. This gesture was so out of character that it surprised me. But I closed my eyes and maintained the embrace with equal resolve. When she disengaged, she pushed me away, as if she had suddenly become uncomfortable with this unusual show of emotion; I nearly lost my balance.

Mrs. Ricci glanced around the living room with that scrutinizing eye of hers. "It looks so clean in here, Ann Marie. Thank you."

Feeling awkward and uncertain about what to do next, I retired to

Derek's room.   Perhaps this wounded family would like some time without me around?   I was considering walking over to Pam's house when I heard a knock on the bedroom door.

"Ann Marie?" came Mr. Ricci's voice.

"Sir?"

He knelt by the bed and pulled out the bundle I had just put there. Without a word, he unwrapped the jacket from a folded American flag and clutched against his heart, this symbol of his son's brave service. Then he handed it to me, asking that I stash it in Derek's closet.

I opened the closet after Mr. Ricci had left the room, reaching up to reverently place the flag onto the top shelf.

A few articles of Derek's clothing still hung there, and for the first time, I noticed his navy-blue karate gi nestled against one of my skirts.

Chapter 20:

NAS ALAMEDA

In June of 1968, the Ricci family put their house up for sale. Jessica Ricci would complete her elementary teaching degree at Cal State Hayward by the end of summer.

The Riccis were kind enough to ask if I wanted to move to New York with them. This surprised me. While I deeply appreciated their kindness in allowing me to live in their home, I had never felt fully comfortable there. Jessica and her mother bickered frequently. Mrs. Ricci was the chief instigator of these spats; I felt that she was hard on her daughter. Mr. Ricci, whose presence might have made things better, worked two jobs and was absent most of the time. Kinder than Mrs. Ricci, he had seemed to placate his wife to keep her in good humor, even before Derek's death. And they were all solemn folks; I can't remember ever hearing a hearty laugh under that roof.

All things considered, a level of tension existed in the Ricci household, which, though infinitely subtler than that in my own home, was nonetheless very real. More than anything else, that kept me from accepting their offer. Still, I was touched by it, and I will never forget their generosity in allowing a perfect stranger into their home.

Given my family's exodus to Arizona, I fretted about where I would live for my senior year. I decided to call Mrs. Etrium, who was technically still the social worker for the McCusker case. My hope was to give her an update on my family, as well as seek out any ideas she might have about where I could live.

Mrs. Etrium seemed genuinely delighted to hear from me. She asked what news I had of the McCusker clan, as it had been months since she had heard anything. Her letters had been returned with no forwarding address. Unable to contact anyone in the family, she had put our case on hold, meanwhile having plenty to do helping other families.

I updated Mrs. Etrium on what I'd been up to, ending by telling her where I was living and my need to move in a few months. "Had you contacted me earlier," said Mrs. Etrium, "I would have authorized the Ricci family to receive funding for you as their foster child."

"But that would've meant telling you why I chose to leave home," I replied. "Which could have resulted in my brothers and sisters being taken away again. And they would rather live where they are than in foster homes." As I spoke, I felt my throat tighten. My mother had had the capacity to change all of that after we suffered through the terror of the courts and the Cottage. But she hadn't. She had allowed my father to return.

"Ann Marie, what about the Donohue family? They were so kind to you in the past, and perhaps now they would be willing to have you live with them on a less transient basis. They would receive a monthly check from the state. It's not much, but enough to cover the added expenses of having another person in the household. You would also have a clothing allowance." She went on to outline the details and summed up by asking me if it would be helpful for her to call the Donohues on my behalf.

"Yes, of course! Thank you so much, Mrs. Etrium."

This woman was the angel I needed at that point in my life, and with her encouragement the Donohues agreed to this plan. Mrs. Etrium made all of the arrangements for me to move in with my best friend's family again, and would later play an instrumental role in finding funding for college – but college was the last thing on my mind at the time. I was in survival mode, needing not only a place to live but also a way to earn money. Mrs. Etrium had furnished the first; the second would come through my high school.

I was one of four students from Mount Eden selected to participate in the summer employment program at the Naval Air Station (NAS) Alameda. I had no idea how we were chosen. I don't remember asking about this, assuming that it had something to do with my being poor, needy, and having family issues.

Our high school counselor arranged a meeting for the four of us in his office, shortly before school got out for the summer. I arrived first and took a seat in his waiting room. Then two guys walked in and sat down. I recognized both as being in my graduating class.

Juan said to his buddy, Guillermo, *"Crees que esa chica esta aqua por le mismo trabajo que nosostros? No es possible."*

After three years of high school Spanish, I understood. Juan wondered if I was there for the same reason as they were. And I was delighted that he had added, "This is not possible." Perhaps I had managed to present myself at school as a reasonably well-off person.

"If you guys are here about working at the Naval Air Station, that's why I am here too," I told them.

Next to walk in was Denise Lloyd. *Are you kidding?* I thought. Dee-Dee was one of the most popular girls in the entire school – varsity cheerleader, student body president and widely recognized as very smart. Could this outstanding student suffer from a troubled home life, like me? *No es possible!*

Mr. Van Slyke opened his office door and invited us in. He explained what was in store for us.

"Mount Eden was a bit late submitting students' names, so we received only four billets. Many of the three thousand seniors participating are from Oakland, and all of you are from the East Bay. Your first forty-hour week will consist of nothing but tests, so the program directors will know where to assign you. There will be a hearing test, but most will be written assessments. The bulk of the available jobs are washing airplanes, working in the civilian cafeteria, stuff like that. But about five percent of you, that is, about 150, will have the opportunity to train in a vocation that you may well use for the rest of your lives."

Mr. Van Slyke was kind enough to help us plan how we would get to and from the air station. Among us, only Juan had a car. He agreed to provide the transportation if we three contributed gas money.

I will never forget those early morning rides. In school, the four of us were in different social circles. In the car, Dee-Dee and I sat in the back, with Juan at the helm and Guillermo in front. The normal social barriers of high school suspended, our initial awkwardness melted away within a few days. We listened to rock and roll, we sang, we laughed, and thoroughly enjoyed our time together.

During those drives up to Alameda and back, I learned about the ease of being teenagers without the pressure of responding to social cliques. None of us would have dreamed of hanging out together at Mount Eden, but here we were not under the watchful eyes of our peers. There were no ethnic boundaries, no need to impress one another because we all knew that we shared a common bond: we came from poor families. The biggest surprise in that department was Dee-Dee, whom we had all assumed came from an upper-middle-class family. It turned out that she sewed her own stylish clothing, and that her father was an alcoholic, like mine.

NAS Alameda was an impressive place to a seventeen-year-old girl. The constant roar of jets taking off and landing, the bustle and excitement of an aircraft carrier deploying or returning, the snappy way Marine guards saluted your vehicle at the front gate – suddenly we were in a world unknown to most civilians. During my time on the base, I would grow to feel honored and privileged to be a part of the activity there, supporting our sailors and soldiers . . . this despite my belief that as a nation, we were sending our young men to die for a cause that was not ours, in Viet Nam.

True to what we had been told, all of us high school students spent our first week taking tests. The first day was medical, which mostly consisted of a lengthy hearing exam. We were told that a post-test would be required to ensure that none of us had suffered hearing loss due to the proximity of jet engines. Four days of paper-and-pencil tests followed, including basic skill and vocational assessments. The last two days included military aptitude tests. The overall objective was to match our skills, interests, and aptitudes to an appropriate job on base.

Our assignments were doled out on Monday morning of the second week. We each received a packet including a map of the base, informing us where to report and to whom. Many of us had civilian supervisors, but some had Navy or Marine Corps supervisors. My paperwork instructed me to report to the Dental Clinic on the second floor of the Dispensary, and ask for Chief Petty Officer Howes.

I was thrilled to be working with sailors. My father had joined the Navy when he was seventeen years old during the Second World War. He spoke about his four years of service with pride and reverence, and a favorite family pastime had long been hearing his war stories. As I followed my map toward the Dispensary, I inquired of a sailor to be sure that I was headed in the right direction.

"Yes, ma'am, you are. Can't miss it, as it overlooks the Parade Ground."

"Thank you. May I ask another question? What is a dispensary? Obviously, a place where something is dispensed, but my assignment mentions a dental clinic and . . . "

The young sailor's friendly laugh interrupted me. He shook his head and said, "Dispensary means hospital. The first floor and most of the second are medical. The rest of the second floor is dental."

He walked me to the steps of the Dispensary. We passed several officers en route and each time my companion stopped short and snapped a crisp salute. Before we parted, he asked for my phone number, suggesting that he might like to take me out on a date. Wow, was I ever was going to love working at this place!

Juan, Guillermo, Denise, and I met later at a designated location for the drive home, all eager to share what we had learned about our new jobs. Everyone tried to speak at once until Denise took charge. "Okay, one at a time! You start, Guillermo."

"Okay, ladies and gentlemen, I am going to learn to be a Zeus (sic) chef, which means that when the big shots have to stay on their boats, I help cook their food."

We all clapped appreciatively.

"Juan?"

"Yeah, so I get to help fix airplanes. Cool, huh? There's one called an A-6 that has its own hanger. Okay, so today maybe I just got to wash a few, but if I do good, I get to help the mechanics."

More applause. "Okay, Annie, you next," said Dee-Dee.

"My job will be to help a dentist fix teeth. Once this guy trains me, I may be able to assist the dentist all by myself. They said it is a job that I could do even after I leave the base. So maybe I will be a dental assistant after I graduate, folks."

"Okay, now my turn," said Denise. "I am working in telecommunications. Not sure about the details yet, but I am going to learn how to use a Teletype, which is how the Navy communicates with ships at sea. I'm not sure if I want to do that for a career since I want to go to college. But, yeah, I think I'm going to like it."

"And let's not forget another bonus, people," added Guillermo. "We can shop at the commissary while we work here."

"Yes, let's not forget another bonus," I added. "I already got asked out." Juan gave Denise an exaggerated look of disapproval, as if warning her against similar adventures – those two had already begun to get a little flirty with one another.

Although it was only fifteen miles from Hayward to Alameda, traffic was heavy and our commutes that summer gave the four of us time to bond in the car. These rides were always joyful, full of laughter and gaiety. We'd share stories about our day and sing along to the radio, imitating the vocalists. Denise could always put the rest of us in stitches with her exaggerated rendition of "Suzie Q."

Lieutenant Hinman and Commander Cagel were the dentists in my new unit. Their assistant was DT2 (Dental Technician, Second Class) Weist. Weist was a wonderful instructor, slowly turning procedures over to me when he thought I was ready. I began with simple things like preparing the amalgam (tooth filling), passing cotton rolls, determining syringe size, and sitting with the patient until the Novocain took effect. I enjoyed chatting with these young sailors – and flirting, if they were cute.

At one point after I'd been there for three weeks, Weist removed his facemask, nodded to the Lieutenant, and left the room. I understood this to mean that I was ready to assist on my own. Naturally, we could not have discussed this in front of a patient, so following Weist's lead, I nodded to the Lieutenant, took Weist's chair, put on a fresh face mask and gloves, and tried to hide the fact that my hands were shaking. But by then I had indeed learned enough to competently assist; within a day or two, I even began to pass appropriate instruments before being asked and anticipated my various duties during the procedures. It surprised me to have become so proficient in such a short time, but then I had had a fabulous teacher.

Officially, Weist was to remain on deck to supervise me. In fact, though, he sometimes left the dispensary altogether at these times, but he mostly lingered around the x-ray department, where his sweetheart Jesse worked.

Jesse had the whitest teeth I had ever seen in my life – a real bonus in a dental clinic (everyone who worked there brushed their teeth after even one morsel of food, and could often be seen with floss hanging from their teeth in between patients). Jesse was the only person we addressed by her first name. She was a standout, not only as the one who could get an x-ray perfectly aligned every single time but also as stunningly beautiful. I loved her name so much that she inspired me to name my daughter Jessica, should I ever have one (and much later, I did).

I began each day at Alameda NAS by standing with the enlisted personnel at 0745 hours for muster. While part of me got a kick out of this ritual – standing at attention, standing at ease, being addressed as "McCusker," and getting nervous when Captain Charm (his real name) made his rounds – I took it quite seriously, overall. Some days I had to remind myself that I was in fact a civilian and not an enlisted member of the United States Navy.

One particular morning during muster, Chief made his usual generic announcements: who was on duty for the evening, which was absent on leave, and such. His last remarks were, "Weist, you assist in your unit. McCusker, you are in Exam today. Dismissed!"

I felt a flutter of nervous excitement. Previously, I had only assisted for Lieutenant Hinman, the more easygoing of the unit's two dentists. Commander Cagel had a reputation for blitzing through procedures, going so fast that a mistake on his assistant's part was almost inevitable. Not only was I still new to the game, being in Exam as opposed to the surgical room would mean charting – taking down rapid-fire information about a patient's teeth. Would I be able to hold my own?

As I headed towards Exam to prepare for my first patient, the Supply Officer, DT1 Brooks, stopped me. He was a tall, thin black guy, and a clear favorite amongst the young techs who were doing their four-year commitment before returning to civilian life. Brooks was *cool*, and he knew it. He also enjoyed saying shocking things. One time he told me (for no apparent reason I can remember) that, "If you put a bean in a jar for every time you get it on during your first year of marriage, then take a bean out every time after that, you won't run out of beans."

Like the other three first-class petty officers in the clinic, Brooks was going to be in the Navy until retirement. I had learned to read the military insignia, and noted from Brooks' three stripes that he'd already had at least twelve years in.

"Hey, you ready to chart in Exam with Cagel?" Brooks asked me on this particular morning.

"Never done it for real, but I practiced with Weist."

"This dude is a prick. It's okay to slow him down. He be hatin' this job cuz he has appointments every fifteen minutes, unlike them other lazy cats. You dig?"

"Yeah, Brooks, I dig."

Encouraging advice from a guy as cool as Brooks helped me keep my head on straight heading into Exam that morning, and the next few hours were indeed a whirlwind, finally interrupted by lunch.

Over the noon hour, the clinic was normally vacant save for one enlisted person on duty and one officer. Their meals were delivered to a small mess hall in the dispensary, along with those for the medical personnel on duty. If I managed to have a dollar or so on me, I would walk to the civilian cafeteria. On this day, I'd packed a sandwich, an apple, and a couple of cookies from 'home'. I'd gone to the enlisted lounge and just opened my lunch sack, when Weist, who was on duty, entered the room and plopped down beside me on the ancient couch.

"How's Exam going, Ann Marie?"

"Cagel goes so fast . . . MODFL #2, refer to OS . . . DO #5 . . ."

Weist shrugged. "It's just a chart. Next, the patient sees a dentist for fillings, who will redo the exam to decide which work they want to do."

I returned to my unit, doubly encouraged to keep doing my best.

At 15:50, our last patient left Exam. But a shameful fact about myself had been bumping around in my head for most of the day, and quickly, before Commander Cagel could even get this mask off, I said, "Sir, could you do an exam on me?"

"Can't do that legally. You're a civilian. Don't you have a dentist?'

"Sir . . . I've never been to the dentist."

Cagel picked up the intercom and called the desk.

"Ginny, who is the duty officer this evening?"

"Weist, sir."

"Tell him to report to Exam. We have a last-minute patient to take care of."

Chapter 21:

ONE FLEW EAST, THE REST STAYED WEST

(WHILE DAD REMAINED IN HIS CUCKOO'S NEST)

In July of 1968, I was at long last enjoying a life free of trauma. My sources of stress consisted of regular teenage stuff, like worrying about how folks at the Dental Clinic would perceive me once they learned that I was a dental assistant who had never been to the dentist myself. Or the conundrum of wanting to date, yet being conservative and feeling somewhat shy around boys.

In the days following my confession to Commander Cagel, nobody at the clinic mentioned anything about my dental history. What a relief. I wanted these people to like me and sought their approval.

Thursday rolled around, and as I prepared for Field Day (a weekly afternoon of deep-cleaning the unit), Weist grinned and told me, "I'm taking over here, so you can report to x-ray now. It's all been worked out, so go immediately." I never worked in the x-ray unit myself and wondered if Jesse was going to film my mouth. If the techs had conspired to do what I thought they might, I was worried for all of us. Treating a civilian in the clinic was taboo. Everyone could get in a lot of trouble.

The commanding officer of the dental unit, Captain Charm, would occasionally show up on Thursday afternoons. Holding his pipe with his teeth and puffing away, hands behind his back, he would walk from unit to unit without saying a word. He was intimidating and ubiquitous, and I'd already gotten in trouble with him once, for working on my homework as I waited in my unit for a patient's mouth to get numb. Hopefully, the Captain would not make an appearance today, of all days.

Jesse did indeed do a full-mouth x-ray, then ushered me off to the tech, who cleaned teeth. The cleaning unit was next to the reception area and easily visible from there. Dawn, a civilian hygienist employed by the Navy, had on this occasion moved her instruments into the surgery unit, which was in the farthest corner of the Clinic. Clearly, this was meant to draw as little attention as possible, as the reception area was busy even on a field day. And should the Captain walk in, he would arrive through the front, leaving ample time for someone to send a warning back to surgery.

It took Dawn almost two hours to clean my teeth. By that time, Jesse had my x-rays developed and displayed on the screen. Touched, grateful, and in awe that these folks would do this for me, I sent up a little request for blessings on their behalf.

Months later, when I lived in my 'foster home', Mrs. Donohue convinced their family dentist to work on my teeth at a discounted rate. At that time, the state did not pay for dental care for foster children unless it was an emergency. I paid Dr. Staley five dollars a month for my entire senior year.

About three weeks after my family skipped town, I received a letter from my mother, sent to the Donohues. In it, Mom told me that she had been against this sudden, unexpected move to Arizona, but Dad had insisted. He had known that I visited the family when he was not around and worried that I might rat him out for drinking, not working, and generally being his usual loser self.

I thought about my family often, but it was easy to put them out of my mind the rest of the time because contact was so infrequent. They had no phone, and Mom's few letters held little detail. I knew only that they were in Phoenix living in a two-bedroom trailer without air conditioning. I could only imagine the misery of ten of them in a small trailer, with Dad. *That* got to me.

In early August, I received a letter from my sister, Kathy, describing my family's life in Arizona. My father had found a job at a used car lot, but food and money were scarce. Their dismal living situation, as well as the intense heat, made everyone irritable and on edge, especially my father. The manager of a small grocery gave them credit, but they soon accumulated a large bill, and Kathy was worried.

I made $218.00 per month at NAS and gave the Riccis $100.00. After receiving the letter from Kathy, I began to send my family a monthly money order for $50.00. Once I'd paid Juan for gas, I was left with very little discretionary income. But it was not lost on me that unlike my siblings, I enjoyed pleasant living conditions and good, regular meals.

I moved in with the Donohue family in late August, as the Riccis prepared for their return to New York. It thrilled me to think that their nice neighborhood on Tulip Avenue would be my home for the next fourteen months. I savored everything about living with this family, with the amazing added bonus of sharing a bedroom with my very best friend, and their reliable routine was a particular comfort. Dinner was always served at five-thirty, and inevitably followed by Mr. Donohue telling his wife, "Ruby Irene, you've done it again!" Everyone in the family had their own chores, so Pam and I did house cleaning on Saturday. This did not seem like a chore to me. I had been accustomed to living in an untidy home, so the difficulty here of finding one small smudge to suck up with the vacuum cleaner felt almost comical. "There, you nasty piece of lint, take that!"

In September, just before school started, I received an envelope containing letters from both Mom and Kathy. They had been evicted from their place in Phoenix and had headed on to Tucson, where my dad's brother, Uncle 'Whitey' lived. They had all moved into my uncle's one-bedroom apartment, while my father looked for work. Mom's letter went on to tell how Kathy, Tom, and Ed had contracted hepatitis A and were violently ill. The apartment did have air conditioning, but no pool. A pool had enabled my siblings to endure the unbearable heat in their previous paltry residence. Now, twelve people in a one-bedroom apartment? With sick kids?

Then I read Kathy's letter, which added to my gut-wrenching dismay. She begged me for help, asking me for bus fare to "come home." Where did she think home was for her, and just how could I help? I wanted to not be reminded of this. *Just let me go about my business and leave me alone!*

Naturally, I was incapable of sustaining any emotional distance from my family. After reading those letters, I hastened to the living room, interrupting Mr. and Mrs. Donohue, who had been watching the evening news.

"May I speak with you for a moment?" I asked.

"What is it, Annie Rooney?" said Mr. Donohue.

"I need to use your phone for a couple of long-distance calls," I said, and then went on to outline a plan for helping Kathy. I would call my Aunt Bernadine to see if Kathy could live with them. "It may take a few calls to work out the details," I finished, "but I'll pay you back."

The Donohues agreed. Feeling grateful for this chance to make a positive difference, I dialed NA9-8887, a number I'd had memorized since our family left New Jersey.

I'd forgotten, though, about the three-hour time difference, and when my cousin Sharon answered, she told me that her parents were in bed, as it was 9:20 PM there. Then I heard a sleepy voice cut in. Aunt Dean must have picked up their bedroom extension.

"Hello? Ann Marie? What the hell is going on? My brother again?"

"Hi, Aunt Bernadine! I need some help."

An extensive conversation followed, which Mr. and Mrs. Donohue could not have helped hearing. When I finally put down the phone, Mr. Donohue stood and walked over to me. Standing behind me, his hands on my shoulders, he said, "You know, Annie, the best way for you to help your family is to help yourself. Be somebody. Get a good job. Show your brothers and sisters it can be done."

I knew that he was right, and I found comfort in his words. But it would take years for me to fully appreciate his advice. Being young and impatient, I wanted to make their lives better NOW.

And such things were not impossible. Within one week, my sister was in Williamstown, New Jersey, and enrolled in Williamstown High School.

God bless you, Aunt Dean.

One down, seven to go.

By September of 1968, Pam and I anxiously anticipated our senior year at Mount Eden. There was so much to look forward to, especially in those magical final months - senior pictures, graduation announcements, cutting school for the first time, the senior talent show, ordering our caps and gowns . . . but most of all, hopefully being asked by a boy to the senior ball. Neither Pam nor I had a boyfriend, and I worried that we would miss the event. I wondered if a couple of the sailors from the Dental Clinic might escort us.

As excited as I was about school, I was not ready to give up the coolest job in the world, so I dropped by the NYC office on base to ask about the possibility of staying on part-time throughout the school year. Pam and I had discussed this, and she was also willing to work at NAS Alameda if we could work together. Plus, I had no car of my own, but Pam was using her brother's car while he served in Viet Nam, so she could provide wheels.

Pam had listened to my stories about working on the base, and my excitement had piqued her interest. But her family did not meet the low-income requirements for NYC. So, it seemed to be a long shot, but worth a try. Surprisingly, the NYC coordinator made that happen with no forms to complete, and no testing for Pam, simply making the comment, "She is your ride, correct? The folks in the dental dispensary want to keep you on, and they trust your judgment, so she's in!"

Since Pam and I had both attended summer school the year before (in my case to be around Derek Ricci), we had plenty of extra credits toward graduation. Thus, we were able to attend school in the morning, and then head out to the base for three hours of work in the afternoon. Pam caught on quickly, and it was not long before she assisted her assigned dentist alone. Like me, she had little experience in the dating world and felt thrilled to be in the company of so many young sailors.

By the end of October, in fact, our potentially romantic interests had entirely shifted from high school guys to the United States Navy. We played it safe by only going to group activities. Pam, our high school buddy, Terry, and I 'dated' various sailors, all six of us packing into Pam's brother's car. Sometimes we took Terry's car, a blue 1959 Impala, which she shared with her younger brother. We'd go bowling or take in a movie, or go for a hike in Cull Canyon in the hills just north of Hayward.

Looking back, I realize how naive and 'square' we girls were. The hippie movement was in full swing in the Bay Area. The likes of Cream, Led Zeppelin, Jimmy Hendricks, and Janice Joplin played regularly at the Filmore in San Francisco. But we couldn't have cared less about that scene. Our style was more The Association, The Carpenters, Tower of Power, and a group called the Jackson Five. Sometimes when I look back, it feels as though I allowed an amazing era, indeed, historical movement, to pass me by. But that's who I was at the time. Unlike so many kids our age, Pam and I were viewed as good girls by our peers, and as exemplary by our elders.

One night, in early November of 1968, Terry called asking if we wanted to do something "fun for once." She sounded excited that since her brother would have 'their' car, her father was going to allow her to use his car. Terry's father was retired from the Navy and had a sticker on his front bumper which allowed the vehicle access past the gate at any naval facility.

"So, we could get into the enlisted club at the naval hospital in

Oakland. I went with my sister last week. I swear, there are ten sailors to every girl, and you won't believe this, but they don't even check I.D.," Terry told me. "My sister and I met so many guys, Ann Marie. We didn't even have to pay for one single drink because guys kept sending them to our table. We danced until the place closed."

"So where is this place? Is it a base, or what?"

"No, it is part of a hospital called Oaknoll, and full of sailors. It's in the Oakland hills off Mac Arthur Boulevard. The guys who are really sick aren't allowed there, so mostly it is recovering sailors and corpsmen waiting to get back out to their ships."

"I don't know," I said. "Doesn't sound like something Pam would want to do, and I doubt her mom would agree. But I would like to go. I'll talk to Pam and get right back to you."

"Just don't tell her mom where we are going. Tell her we're going to a movie. Pick you guys up at eight. You don't need to call me back unless you can't go. Bye, Annie!"

I was thrilled, but as expected, Pam was not up for it. "This sounds dangerous, if not illegal, and my parents would never agree," she said. "We are underage to go to a place like that."

Normally if I begged Pam to do something, she would relent. But not this time. So, lying to her parents about where I was going, I headed out with Terry the next night.

Marines saluted as we passed through Oaknoll's guarded gate without incident. We parked, then walked into a crowded, smoke-filled enlisted lounge. Terry and I sat at one of the few vacant tables, and within seconds, we were joined by four men. Terry immediately began to flirt in a suggestive manner, which made me uncomfortable. I knew right then that I'd made a mistake.

Someone at the table bought drinks for Terry and me. This was only the second alcoholic drink I'd ever had in my life, and the guy handing it my way asked if Rum-and-Coke was okay. When I nodded yes, he asked me to dance.

Credence Clear Water Revival's *Proud Mary* was blasting so loudly that it was impossible to talk as we walked to the tiny dance floor, where my partner immediately pulled me close. Unfortunately for me, that tune ended just as we got there, followed by a slow dance. When the guy started grinding against me, I pushed him away and went back to the table. I could see Terry's dance partner was acting just as mine had, but she seemed to enjoy it. At that point, it became clear to me that I just wanted to get out of there and go home.

I planned to ask Terry if we could leave once she returned to the table. I knew that she would be upset. As she stayed on the dance floor for at least half a dozen more songs, I realized it was going to be difficult to get home without a quarrel. Meanwhile, guys kept asking me to dance. I kept refusing. It felt as though my very presence in the place implied my willingness to be sexual. I felt awkward and way out of my league. I caught Terry's eye once and gestured for her to come back to the table. She waved at me and kept on dancing. *Big mistake coming here*, I told myself.

I stood and looked around for the restroom, finally spotting a sign that simply read "Heads" far across the dance floor. Walking toward it, I grabbed Terry's arm, and said, "Come to the bathroom with me – please!" She managed to extricate herself from some sailor's tight hold and followed me.

Before I could get a word out in the safer confines of the ladies' room, Terry said, "What the heck is the matter with you, Ann Marie?"

"I hate it here. I want to go home. Terry, can we please leave? Every guy here is just looking for one thing and . . ."

"That why it's so much fun, dummy. Let loose. Have a good time."

"I want to get out of here, Terry!"

She looked at her watch and said, "Okay, okay. Give me an hour.

There's this really cute guy and I just want a little more time so he can ask me for my phone number."

"Give me your keys and I'll wait in the car."

"So, what I am supposed to tell people? I don't want to be all by myself."

I shook my head and gave her a firm look. "One hour."

She left the ladies room, and I lingered. On my way back to the table, I noticed a sign reading, "No drinks beyond this point". That sounded promising. I peered through the door beyond the sign. Outside was a large wooden deck with a couple of chairs and two tables. I didn't see anyone out there. Looking for a place to hide out for an hour, I walked onto the deck.

It was refreshing to get out of the cigarette smoke. The deck was dimly lit and a bit creepy, but it beat being stuck at a table, surrounded by horny sailors.

Oaknoll Naval Hospital was where Viet Nam amputees were stationed to recover and learned to cope with missing limbs. As my eyes adjusted to the low light, I made out a long series of ramps that began several buildings above my location, then zig-zagged down the steep hillside of the hospital grounds. I found myself watching several amputees in wheelchairs ready themselves to race down the ramps. They hollered and yelled, until above the hoopla I heard a voice cry, "Let the race begin!" Then all hell broke loose as six patients in wheelchairs raced down the ramps, hooting, and bellowing out expletives as they went, often leaning back and gliding on the back two wheels of their chairs. It was a joyful moment. I smiled, leaning forward over the railing to get a good view. Lost in thought about how these young men who came home maimed from Viet Nam could be so happy, I jumped when I heard a voice behind me say, "Hello there, beautiful."

Startled, I stood frozen as a tall figure emerged from a shadowed corner of the deck. The stranger dragged two chairs to a spot, which was partially lit by a window. Then, making an exaggerated sweeping gesture with his arm – an offer to be seated – he fell over. After a moment's hesitation, I helped him into one of the chairs. I ended up chatting with this drunken sailor for over an hour. Despite his inebriation, I instinctively felt safe with him – or perhaps I could see that he was too plastered to do anyone any harm.

His name was Thom Walker. He was from Murfreesboro, Tennessee, and a patient at the hospital. Not only did this guy have all of his limbs, he was drop-dead gorgeous, and didn't seem sick in any obvious way. I liked him and wondered what he would be like sober. After Thom and I had been chatting for a while, I realized that Terry would have no idea where I was, so I excused myself and went back into the bar to find her.

She was seated at the same table with a crowd of corpsman and two other women. I stood over her, cupping both my hands over one of her ears in an attempt to be heard over the loud music, letting her know where I'd been. Then I noticed Thom coming inside. He spotted me, came to the table, and took the only vacant seat. I dragged an empty chair to the table and sat down. It was impossible to continue our conversation with the rock and roll drowning us out, so I found myself just looking over at Thom and smiling. *Should I give him my phone number? But what if I saw him again when he was sober, and he realized that I was not the kind of beauty that a guy like him could attract? He may not even remember me in the morning . . .*

"Let's dance," Thom said to me after a few minutes, and he pulled me out onto the floor for a slow number. Thom held me close. He smelled of aftershave and stale beer. He danced with me in a respectful manner, unlike my previous partner, and with sure, steady movements, despite his drunken state.

"Last call," shouted the bartender.

Returning to our table, I noticed Terry passing her phone number to one of the guys. "May I have your phone number?" asked Thom.

With Terry's pen, I wrote the Donohue's phone number on a cocktail napkin and handed it to him.

We all parted outside the enlisted club, but not before Thom grabbed me and gave me the most disgusting kiss I'd ever experienced – not that there had been many. He stuck his tongue so far inside my mouth, I thought I might gag. How sick, I thought. Maybe it would be just fine if I never heard from him again.

Slinking through the front door of the Donohue home in the wee hours of the morning, I wondered what I would say to Mrs. Donohue since I was supposed to have gone to a see the movie "Oliver!" that evening. I was not feeling so swell about lying. *Plus, what will I do if this guy Thom actually does call me?* As I struggled in the dark to get my clothes off, pajamas on, and into bed, Pam's bedside light snapped on. It startled me, even though I should have known that she would wait up for me. We chatted, and I fell asleep not feeling very good about myself for lying to have my night out.

Pam and I awoke at ten the next morning to an empty house, save for Pam's younger sister, Susan. We dragged ourselves into the kitchen for bowls of cereal. Susan mentioned that someone from my family had called collect the night before, but her mother had refused to accept the charges. Minutes later, Mr. and Mrs. Donohue arrived home from grocery shopping. Mrs. Donohue did not quiz me about my evening, but made the point that collect calls from my family would require reimbursement on my part, asking if would I like her to accept the charges next time.

Now I was fretting about two potential calls – worried about what could be up with my family that merited a long-distance call, and wondering if that sailor would follow up. Hardly admitting it even to myself, I hoped that he would.

The Donohue family had two phones: one in the dining/family room and one in the parents' bedroom. At 7:00 P.M. the phone rang, and Mrs. Donohue picked up. "I'm going to take this in our bedroom," she announced, "so someone hang up when I get there."

I watched the clock. By 7:50 PM, I thought that Mrs. Donohue was likely to go on talking forever, so I might as well give up and do my homework. I had just spread my books out on the dining room table when Mrs. Donohue returned, clearly no longer on the phone.

Shortly after 8:00 PM, the phone rang again. I jumped into action, quickly blurting to Mrs. Donohue, "I'll get it. If it's someone from my family calling collect, I will pay." Without waiting for her answer, I picked up.

"Hello," I said, unraveling the long cord, hoping it would stretch into the living room.

"May I please speak with Ann Marie?"

"Speaking," I said, on pins and needles but hoping to sound as nonchalant as possible.

"Hi, Ann Marie. This is Thom Walker. We met last night at the Oaknoll enlisted club?"

"Well hello, Thom." My heart raced, yet I hoped above anything else to make my voice sound casual and relaxed . . . as if this kind of thing happened to me regularly. "Good to hear your voice." *Oh, my gosh, how stupid was that . . .* "How are you?" *Ugh, even more stupid.*

"Well, I have to admit, I was a tad bit hung over this morning. And a wee bit embarrassed because I don't remember a whole heck of a lot about last night." He went on speaking in this friendly manner, and within minutes, I felt at ease. Our conversation became effortless, and I hadn't realized that over an hour had gone by until Mrs. Donohue walked into the living room and told me that it was time to get off the phone.

"Hey Thom, I have to get off the phone. I don't have a car and I assume you don't either, being stationed on a ship, so I need to check with my buddy, Pam, and see if she would be willing to drive me to Oaknoll."

"Okay, so you check with her and I will call you tomorrow?"

"Sounds great," I said.

The next day was a Monday. Pam and I went to school, then to work at the Naval Air station. After dinner, the phone rang, and I sprang up to answer. This time it was my mother, not calling collect. She was more talkative than usual, letting me know that Dad had landed a job at a new car dealership that the kids were all well and in school, although Tom and Ed had just returned there after a bout with Hepatitis A. She added that the kids were sick of changing schools all the time, and being behind in their classes and that they might all be moving back to California in a month. They had landed in a nice three-bedroom apartment, but only after having been evicted from Uncle Whitey's place.

On the day of the eviction, Rosemary had come home from school to find Uncle Whitey's apartment completely empty, except for the furniture that went with the place. Someone had forgotten to fill Rosemary in, so she had returned 'home' after school, but suddenly had no idea where to go, or what to do. I choked back tears, imagining her terror. The poor kid was only ten years old. Fortunately, she had managed to remember where one of my uncle's friends lived; she had gone there, and thank God, he had known where to take her.

Only after we disconnected did I replay the words, "We might be moving back to California next month." Dad had a job, they had a decent place to live, and yet moving back was on the table? It sounded fishy.

My family might be coming back. Mixed emotions tumbled from every corner of my brain. As long as they were far away, I had some amount of peace in my life. Naturally, I worried, but from a distance, there was no role I could actively play. Well, not *no* role – I had helped Kathy get out. But with a great sense of guilt, I found myself hoping that they would retain their distance my life. As if I'd ever had a choice about where the family 'home' was to be.

Chapter 22:

FIRST LOVE

If my sailor was seeking an easy lay, AO2 Walker must have known that I was the wrong choice – so did he hang around because he actually cared? This frankly baffled me and seemed too good to be true. I was well liked at Mount Eden, although my reputation as a 'nice girl' and a 'brain' left me on the sidelines in the romance department. But with a view of me unclouded by my peers' prejudices and my troubled family history, Thom enthusiastically pursued me.

Since it was difficult to find the time or place to be alone with Thom, I would sometimes skip school – for the first time in my life – allowing us to spend hours on the Donohue's couch petting when nobody was home. I was hopelessly, madly, joyfully in love – and yet, being a serious and sensible young woman, never allowed myself to go past a certain point, physically or verbally.

Ah, first love! I fluttered around Mount Eden like an untethered balloon. I could scarcely concentrate on senior lit– or any other class – daydreaming about Thom's big brown eyes. I found myself laughing more freely, being more friendly, and believing that I had the best life in the entire universe.

As the holiday season approached, Mrs. Donohue told me that I could ask Thom over for Christmas Eve and to spend Christmas Day with us. Naturally, I was giddy with excitement over this, especially when Thom said yes. The Donohue's had been letting me use one of their cars when it was available, so I drove it up to Oaknoll to pick up Thom that Christmas Eve. As I parked outside of his room, he emerged with three beautifully wrapped gifts. He loaded them into the trunk and then, to my surprise, invited me to come inside for a few minutes.

This terrified me. Thom's room was secluded and private. Our petting had become intense, and I worried about us getting carried away. Despite his claims that he was a virgin like me, I wondered. Thom was almost twenty-two years old and had been in the Navy for almost four years . . .

"Thom, they're waiting for us, so they can serve dinner," I said.

The disappointment on his face was obvious. His smile vanished, and he looked down at his feet. Wanting to offer him something, I added, "But you're spending the night, so maybe I could pay you a visit after everyone is asleep." That perked him up, and he agreed – clearly thinking that I suggested far more than I actually was, but at least that quick thinking had gotten me out of a pinch.

Driving back to Hayward, the Turtles tune "Happy Together" came on the radio. I turned up the volume and began singing along, "I can't see me lovin' nobody but you for all my life . . ." I ventured a look at Thom, and his eyes were so tender. He kissed my hand. By this time I had only known him for eight weeks, yet it felt like forever.

At the Donohue's, a delightful aroma greeted us from the kitchen. Our hosts served up ham, scalloped potatoes, fresh string beans with almonds, salad, and French bread, with Pam's favorite chocolate cake for dessert. Thom put his three gifts under the tree. I assumed that they were all for me, and worried that the sweater I'd bought him at Sears was not going to be enough.

Thom brought his great sense of humor to the gathering, and everyone laughed a lot on that Christmas Eve. We played board games, then some pinochle. I don't remember ever spending such a lovely Christmas Eve, so fun and peaceful. Despite the gaiety, though, I felt something missing, and instinctively knew what it was. The ritual, vestments, incense, ceremony, and Latin of Midnight Mass had always comforted me. The possibility of going never came up, however, so I said nothing.

Everyone headed for bed at eleven o'clock. Rather than washing my face, I reapplied my makeup. Thom was on the couch in the living room. At midnight, I had just started to creep out of the bedroom when I heard Pam say, "Going to give Thom a goodnight kiss?"

"Well, yes, I mean, I told Thom I'd, uh, anyway, be back in a few minutes," I said.

Thom was lying on his back, wide-awake. I boldly laid myself on top of him and kissed him. Before long I felt a bulge near his groin. I longed to touch him there, but became self-conscious, particularly given the setting, so I said "Goodnight," returned to my bedroom, and lay wide awake for the rest of the night, content with my fantasies.

Mr. and Mrs. Donohue typically awoke much earlier than the rest of us, and Christmas Day turned out to be no exception. I heard them get up, peeked out the door, and saw them in the kitchen/family room. I had never been with them on Christmas and wondered if it was okay if folks appeared in their pajamas. I hoped so since I'd borrowed money from Pam to buy new pajamas, which I thought looked glamorous. To my dismay, I saw that Mrs. Donohue was fully dressed – pajamas were a no-go.

By the time I got showered, used electric curlers on my hair, and put on my make-up, everyone else was at the kitchen table. Thom and the Donohue parents were drinking coffee. I poured a glass of orange juice and sat down. Pam excused herself to take a shower. I looked carefully at Thom. His brown hair was in disarray, and his beard looked scruffy. I gave him a hug, wishing it could have been a kiss, and blurted out, "So this is what you look like in the morning."

"Don't be vulgar, Ann Marie," snapped Mrs. Donohue. Mr. Donohue stepped in for me, saying, "Well, I agree with you Annie Roonie, he is a handsome lad, even in the morning." *God bless Mr. Donohue*, I thought.

After everyone showered, we ate a breakfast of waffles, eggs, and bacon. I felt pleased and proud that Thom was getting the chance to see me functioning as part of this good family (even though I still felt the sting of Mrs. Donohue's comment).

Then we moved to the living room to open gifts. Artificial trees had just come into fashion, and the Donohues' was made of aluminum foil, with a light shining on it that changed colors. Despite the trendy novelty of it, I missed the wonderful scent of a real Christmas tree.

Thom insisted on distributing his gifts first. He first gave a "family gift" to Mrs. Donohue. It was a spice rack. During a previous visit, Thom had noted that the family didn't have one. I could tell that he had scored bonus points – particularly later, when he mounted it on the kitchen wall. Pam received her own gift from Thom, though I can't remember what it was. His gift to me was a Bulova watch, with several tiny diamonds. I was charmed.

When it was time to drive Thom back to Oaknoll, Mr. Donohue offered me his car. Once back at the hospital, I declined Thom's repeated offer to accompany him to his room. Our romantic life was getting ever steamier, and I was frankly afraid. The desire was there, but my shyness overruled my fantasies. I was not ready for a sexual relationship.

Driving home in Mr. Donohue's car, I hoped that Thom's sexual expectations were not so important to him that I would lose him. To distract myself, I pushed an eight-track tape into the player, and listened to the tune that popped on . . . "Is That All There Is?" by Peggy Lee.

This tune was not helpful. I ejected the tape, and found myself thinking about Mr. Donohue . . . a sweet and quiet man, who seemed content to allow his wife to run the show. I realized that I had never once saw him angry, or heard him raise his voice. Was he happy? Did Peggy's lyrics reflect how he felt about his life? Sadness overcame me. He had always been so kind to me, and my heart swelled with gratitude. How I wished *he* was my dad!

Mr. and Mrs. Donohue seemed to have a nice enough relationship. It did look kind of boring from my teenage viewpoint . . . but at least it was peaceful, and that held tremendous value for me, and hope for the possibilities in my own future.

*** *** ***

Naturally, every serviceman at Oaknoll Naval Hospital was recovering from some illness or injury. Patients who had served in Viet Nam awaited orders to return to their unit or to be discharged from the military. For weeks, I remained mystified as to why Thom was there, and why he was unwilling to share the reason with me – he seemed perfectly normal and had no obvious physical issues. Finally, soon after Christmas, he trusted me enough to give me details.

Thom had been stationed aboard the aircraft carrier U.S.S. *Ranger*. He had worked in ordnance, and often carried trays of adapter boosters to the flight deck in order to arm the five-hundred-pound bombs, which would be loaded onto A-6 aircraft, and later dropped over Viet Nam. One day, while Thom carried one of these trays to the aircraft several decks below, a booster had exploded, with enough force to send him flying. His head had slammed against a metal bulkhead.

Thom went on to explain that he might have sustained a head injury, and Navy doctors had put him through many batteries of neurological tests – but Thom remained evasive when I asked for more detail. Only much later did I learn that he had been having seizures.

The *Ranger* had been deployed to Japan shortly after his accident, and he was to remain at Oaknoll until it returned to its home port – NAS Whidbey Island, up in Washington State. In the meantime, he and I continued to spend as much time together as possible. We traveled all over the Bay Area – often using public transportation, and sometimes accompanied by Pam. But even with a friend along, these excursions were all about *us*, and San Francisco's Coit Tower, with its majestic and romantic view of the city, became *our spot*.

Near the end of January, Thom had to go join his ship. He was to receive his discharge in May, and promised that the moment he did, he would come back to me, even before returning to his hometown of Murfreesboro, Tennessee. The plan was that when the *Ranger* returned to its home port, Thom would catch a military hop from Whidbey to Alameda. My heart fluttered. There was no reason besides me for him to rush back to the Bay Area.

Once Thom was gone, we wrote to one another every single day, and exchanged audio tapes once a week. I felt as though I'd been admitted to a secret society. For the first time, I had an honest-to-God boyfriend.

Whenever I received a tape from Thom, I would anxiously await the moment after dinner when I could retire in private to Pam's and my bedroom. I would plug in the portable tape recorder, kick off my shoes, and sprawl out on the floor to listen.

Thom's tapes were always far more interesting than I imagined mine could ever be. What did *I* have to talk about? High school? But Thom's life aboard the aircraft carrier fascinated me, and his descriptions were fluid and alive. He liked to record while hanging in the protective netting which surrounded the flight deck. While the netting was there to prevent sailors from falling overboard, apparently it was also a favored spot to 'hang out' and be assured of privacy. I laughed aloud when he told me about this, but found it more than simply amusing. That he would perform this forbidden and dangerous act, hanging in netting from the sides of a ship for *me*, magnified my wildly romantic feelings.

I always enjoyed the distinctive background sounds on these tapes. I had imagined that I would hear waves, like one hears while standing at the seashore, but there was nothing like that. Instead, there was engine noise and the constant low-key roar of the ship's bow cutting through a vast sea. Sometimes I had to strain to hear Thom's voice, as the wind muffled his words.

But there was no mistaking the clarity of his voice one particular evening, as I listened to the most recent tape. Thom said, "And now I want to tell you something, Ann Marie. Are you listening carefully? I love you. Do you hear me? I love you Ann Marie McCusker, and I am coming home to YOU! God, I hope you love me, too. So, finally, I am signing off with what has been in my heart for some time now. I love you."

I rewound that portion of the tape, and listened to it again . . . and again . . . and again. Finally, I went into the Donohue's family room where Pam was watching television with her parents. There must have been quite the look on my face, and I imagine that my cheeks were flushed because Pam was on her feet instantly.

"What? What did he say?"

I gestured for her to follow me, and once we were in our bedroom, I closed the door and squealed, "He loves me!"

At that point, in spite of my feelings for Thom and the flowering of our relationship, I had never once told him, "I love you." But hearing those words from him meant the world to me, and I resolved to share my own feelings at the soonest opportunity.

Thom's profession of love helped steady me, enough that I finally felt ready to follow up on a phone call I'd received from my mother, a few days after he had shipped out. She'd called with big news – my family was back in Hayward, and had been since Christmas! Although anxious to see my brothers and sisters, I had put off committing to a visit, due to the possibility of seeing my Dad. Now, I called Mom and promised that I would catch a bus after work the next day, and come to see them.

I was distracted all morning at school and even more so at work. Before leaving the dental clinic that afternoon, I emptied several cleaning instruments from the autoclave into my purse. I added cotton swabs, alcohol wipes, and a small bottle of mercury (used in those days to make the amalgam for fillings). Carrying those items, plus several candy bars, and some nickels and dimes, I hopped off the bus within a few blocks of Chisholm Court, the new McCusker residence. They were on the second floor of an apartment complex.

I held my breath as I knocked. My siblings and my Mom would be thrilled to see me, but I was not so sure about my Dad.

To my relief, Dad was out looking for a job. I greeted each and every one of my brothers and sisters with a hug, tears of happiness coursing down my face. During this joyous reunion, I noticed a set of Arizona license plates on the dining room table. When I asked about them, Mom told me that they belonged to the vehicle in the carport, the one they had driven back to California.

"Dad took the bus rather than use the car? Why?"

"Um, I can't say for sure," replied my Mom.

While my suspicions were raised, I didn't spend too much time wondering what Dad was up to . . . there was so much catching up to do with my mother and siblings. Only months later did I learn that my father had *stolen* the car from the sales lot where he'd worked in Tucson, justifying this criminal act by claiming that he needed to get the family out of the Arizona heat. I also learned from Kathy that he had stolen a blank check from someone in Arizona and used it to buy Christmas gifts for the whole family. Kathy recalled that the trunk of the stolen car had been filled with presents, and my siblings had awoken on Christmas morning to extravagant gifts. My father obsessed about providing for his family on Christmas Day. In his eyes, this defined him as a good parent, regardless of the ultimate consequences.

Without Dad's presence, the reunion was delightful. The younger kids had grown so much! I learned that they had all been in California for weeks before contacting me, crowded into a sleazy hotel room in Oakland. My father had not allowed anyone to call me. Surely he had been worried that I would notify the state. Little did he know that I would have thought long and hard before doing that. The last time I'd taken such a stand, it had resulted in nothing but trauma for my siblings. I no longer believed that my mother could be strong enough to strike out on her own. I had learned that it was best to remain silent on the subject of my family's whereabouts.

After the initial burst of hugs and kisses, I opened my purse, removed the dental instruments, and got to work. One by one, I began cleaning each sibling's teeth. The kids never balked, going right along with their bossy sister's agenda. It thrilled me to do something so concrete for them. I did not have the means to rescue them from their miserable family life, but I sure as heck could clean their teeth! How ironic that I followed up that activity by distributing candy bars.

For my grand finale, I dug through the bottom of my purse, gathered the nickels and dimes, and spread the coins on the kitchen table. Then I removed the bottle of mercury, and put two drops in each one of their hands, as well as my own. I picked up a tarnished nickel and rubbed the mercury into it. With widening eyes, my brothers and sisters did the same. They marveled over how shiny and new-looking the coins became. Each of them got to keep one dime and one nickel. Today, of course, that sort of mercury magic would be viewed as too dangerous for kids, but we had an amazing time.

I found myself taking a long and appraising look at my brothers. Tom, Ed, Jim, and Bill had all let their hair grow past their shoulders. I didn't think that this had much to do with the late-sixties trend of boys wearing their hair longer, guessing that family finances were probably behind it. And *everyone's* clothing looked as though it could use a good wash. I imagined that their exit from Arizona must have been hasty, so most likely my siblings only possessed the clothes on their backs.

Checking the watch that Thom had given me for Christmas, I told the gang that it was nearly time for my bus. The two youngest, Trish and Bernadine, began to cry. I reassured them that they would see me at least once a week. I hugged each one of those tanned kids and left.

As I walked back to the bus stop, it struck me that I had hardly interacted with my mother. I felt different about her now, in a way that

I couldn't find words for. I was happy to have them all back in my life . . . or *was* I? Already I felt that powerless sense of worry settling back over me. It was wonderful to be heading back to the Donohue home, where life was normal, safe, and predictable. But that invading ache was back because my improving life was not the life that my siblings had, and I couldn't do a darn thing about it.

As I waited for my bus, another one pulled up across the street. There was no mistaking the man who got off. It was my father. I covered my face with my hand, peering at him between my fingers. He walked briskly in the direction of Chisholm Court. I wasn't tempted to call out to him and only watched as his slender figure disappeared into the distance.

I very much wanted to talk with Thom about these events, and the feelings they stirred in me but felt afraid of overwhelming him. I had given him only scanty information about my family life, just enough to satisfy his curiosity about why I lived with the Donohues. Worried that he might judge me, I had decided to fill him in slowly, over time.

There was no denying it – the more I saw of how other families functioned, the more ashamed I became of my own background. Only a week before, the Mount Eden attendance sheets had begun to list my name as Ann Marie Donohue. To this day I have no idea how that error occurred, but I do remember how seriously I considered *keeping* that last name. The idea of having a whole new identity was appealing. It took days of indecision before I finally decided to go to the high school office, and inform them I had not been adopted, or whatever it was they thought. My last name was, still, McCusker.

Chapter 23:

FAKE IT UNTIL YOU MAKE IT

After the visit with my family at Chisholm Court, I was surprised by how easily I resumed my life apart from them. I reverted instantly to being just another girl in love. An involved high school senior. A dental assistant who loved her job. I felt intelligent, full of power to choose the life I wanted.

For years I had watched, emulated, and integrated. In earlier visits to friends' houses, I had observed how other people lived – how often they bathed, their use of napkins, their clean bedding with a top sheet, and more than a single thin blanket. Later, I became more aware of how people behaved socially, how they presented themselves to others. Sometimes I felt fake as I copied what they did, wondering if their way of life would ever become natural for me.

The Guidance staff at Mount Eden began urging seniors to plan for our future after graduation. My buddy Shari and I had talked about college, way back in junior high. One of our favorite pastimes had been to climb up onto her flat roof on La Porte Street and watch Cal State Hayward being built, up in the Hayward hills. Shari would often comment, "One day, I'm going to that school." "Me too," I responded blithely, more than once. And yet college had never been a topic of discussion in my family.

My life still felt defined by questions of day-to-day survival. It felt as if I could, at any moment, find myself without a place to live, and the effort involved in finding and applying for a college didn't seem to fit into such an uncertain scenario. I had taken the SAT exam the year before – goaded into it my Mr. Van Slyke, my guidance counselor – and scored modestly high. But my vision for the future was quite clear: after graduation, I would find work as a full-time dental assistant. I would save some money, and marry Thom Walker in a few years.

A good job. A desirable husband. *A normal life*. It all sounded mighty appealing to me. But that was before I found out what an active interest Mr. Van Slyke had been taking in my future.

Months before, he'd asked me to write an essay for the California State Scholarship Commission, and I had. I don't remember the topic, let alone my response to it. Being a serious student, I did what I was told.

Then one day, out of the blue, Mr. Van Slyke called me into his office and greeted me with an enormous grin on his round face. "Congratulations, young lady!" he said, holding up a large manila envelope. "It's an honor to inform you that you have been selected as one of the California State scholars!"

"Sir?"

He pulled out a paper certificate. "This is a one-thousand-dollar scholarship to the California college of your choice.

I was stunned. This news certainly did jolt the tidy image of my future that I'd put together. To put things into perspective, California's junior colleges were tuition-free in 1969, and state college tuition averaged forty-six dollars per term.

"Are you serious? I never dreamed I would be able to attend college."

I felt a surge of joy over this accomplishment – but also fear. Could I really do this? After all, I really had just made myself up. I had copied, emulated, performed the necessary roles. Would attempting to succeed as a college student reveal me to the world as the poser I felt myself to be?

"So, Ann Marie, where have you applied?"

"I, uh, I haven't filled out *any* applications," I stammered.

214

"Well, would you like some help with that? Ann Marie, I am *so* pleased for you. This office, your teachers, and I'm sure your friends, all know that you are bright and excellent college material. So, let's start talking about what you'd like to study and where you'd like to go. Have you considered Berkeley?"

I ended up applying to Cal State Hayward, the college on the hill that I had watched being built from my friend's rooftop. Though I started the application to Berkeley, fear choked any efforts to venture beyond my hometown. Besides, I had not ruled out the possibility of becoming a full-time dental assistant after high school. It was important work, and I was good at it. If all else failed, it would enable me to earn a steady income.

A few weeks later, Mr. Van Slyke called me in again. "More good news, Ann Marie! Here's a three-hundred-dollar scholarship from the Hayward Women's Business Association." I had interviewed with that organization a few weeks earlier, at his suggestion. Mr. Van Slyke reminded me to watch the mail for further information about financial aid. Soon I did, in fact, receive notification that I'd qualified for a full package of aid, largely grant money that I wouldn't have to pay back.

On the following Monday morning, after the bell rang at Mount Eden, I caught a city bus that headed up the hill to Cal State. Making a beeline for the same tall building I had watched being built years before, I entered the lobby. It looked fancy and official inside, like a big bank. Exiting quickly, I continued to walk around the campus. It felt huge and intimidating, and at first, I kept my eyes on the ground. After stealing a few glances, though, I finally took a good look around. What I saw around me did not seem scary – students scurrying off to class, others sitting on benches and socializing – maybe not that different from high school. *Okay, perhaps I will go to school here. Need to decide what to study, though.*

The State Scholarship Commission sent a representative to Mount Eden, to take a photo of me and the other recipient from my high school, Cecilia Raybuck. Cecilia was our class valedictorian. I felt honored to be in her league. Our pictures ended up being put on display at Southland Mall, in Hayward. Surprisingly, I learned about this from my mother, who routinely called me once every week from a pay phone.

"Seriously, Mom? My picture's up at the mall!?" I asked.

"Yes, honey," she responded, "and I sure wish all the kids could see it. We only had room in the car for the boys. We were shopping for new shoes." That was good news – it meant that Dad had found gainful employment of some kind.

I learned there would be an official presentation of our scholarships at a gala film premiere in Hayward (The Thomas Crowne Affair), with comic celebrity Red Buttons hosting the ceremony. With Thom away at sea, Pam was to be my escort for the evening.

This event turned out to be far more prestigious – and formal – than I had prepared for. I turned up at the theater to find hundreds of nicely dressed guests milling about in the lobby, drinking champagne and nibbling appetizers. Glancing at a program, I noticed that the evening's benefactors included service organizations, banks, hospitals, and governmental agencies. But then my eyes were drawn to bold lettering at the top – and I discovered that the keynote speaker was to be Ronald Reagan, Governor of California. *No way!*

A woman had written to us scholarship recipients, instructing us to meet her in the lobby. This hostess distributed nametags, corsages, and boutonnieres to the scholars – all of whom, I saw to my dismay, sported suits and ties, or nice cocktail dresses. And there I was, decked out in my modest school clothes. I felt my face redden. How had I not been informed about the formal nature of the event?

Later I would learn that a letter advising scholars on appropriate attire, among other important information, had been sent weeks before, in an envelope addressed: *To the Parents of Ann Marie McCusker.* It had somehow been misplaced, and never opened. Mr. Donohue found it days later, stuck inside one of his Time magazines.

216

Our hostess opened a locked door marked Do Not Enter. She cautioned us scholars to be quiet as we filed in to take seats in the front row. At this point, I had to part ways with Pam – despite wishing that we could sit together since she looked to be the only person there as under-dressed as I was. As we were led down a narrow corridor, I found myself thinking about the countless times in my life when I'd felt the humiliation of poverty – and now, on the most prestigious occasion of my young life, I had managed once again to look like a ragamuffin. *Damn it all!*

By the time we reached our seats, Red Buttons was on stage cracking jokes. Following this comic intro, Governor Reagan gave a speech about the importance of education, and then Mr. Buttons announced that he would begin calling the names of the scholarship recipients. I prayed that we could simply stand up at our seats, and acknowledge the crowd from there. That stage was the last place I wanted to be at that moment.

That was not to be. Red Buttons called out names from various schools across the state, and recipients made their way up to the stage. Mr. Buttons finally said, "And now from Mount Eden High School, right here in Hayward!" He called my name and Cecilia's, and we walked to the stage together. Cameras flashed amidst a round of applause. I relished the sensation of celebrity – but just for a moment, until I remembered what I was wearing. I exited the stage as fast as I could.

Unbeknownst to me, Mrs. Etrium was in the audience. After the event, she found me in the crowd and presented me with a lovely bouquet of flowers. It turned out that Mr. Van Slyke had solicited reference letters from her and had kept her in the loop as to my progress.

We greeted one another with a long hug. After pulling away, I thought I noticed her evaluating my outfit.

"Any news from your family? Last I heard from you, they were in

Arizona."

Of course, I had avoided telling her that they were back in town. I felt myself flush and didn't know what to say.

"We might need to talk . . ." was the best I could manage.

She gave me an uncertain look. "Okaaaaay? Can I drop by the high school?"

"Sure, but can we make it in a week or so? I'm just so busy right now." The truth was, I needed time to think.

Mrs. Etrium was hardly out of earshot when an incredulous Pam said to me, "She doesn't know your family is back in Hayward?"

"Not yet. I guess I should tell her. I just don't want my brothers and sisters to see me as some kind of rat fink . . . not after that last fiasco, which ended up fixing *nothing* and only brought more fear into their lives."

"Look," Pam said, in a firm voice, "that had nothing to do with you. Your Dad messed up – *again* – and your Mom did nothing about it – *again.*"

"Right. So what's the point of saying anything, Pam? If Mrs. Etrium contacts them, they'll just skip town again. At least now I can see them."

When we got back to the Donohue's, we noted that the lights were still on. Pam was concerned. Both of her parents woke early to get to their jobs. "It's past eleven," she said. "They must be waiting up for us." Wordlessly, Pam and I looked at one another and clearly shared the same thought. Her brother Johnny was serving in Viet Nam.

Pam walked into the house first. Following right behind, I heard the dull background noise of the television as we headed for the family room. Mr. Donohue's easy chair was empty. That was a good sign. Mrs. Donohue was on the couch with her hair in rollers, covered by their familiar pink net.

With no prelude whatsoever, she blurted out, "Ann Marie, your sister Patricia was hit by a car late this afternoon. Your mother called this evening and said that they think she may have internal injuries, so they are keeping her. She's at Kaiser Hospital. Tell me how in the name of God any parent could allow a six-year-old child to walk with her five-year-old sister across that busy street!"

Yet again, a momentous evening of personal recognition for me was to be overshadowed by family trauma.

I ran to the phone and searched for the number for Kaiser in the phone book. *I stand with my siblings* - this mantra of mine played over and over again in my head as I dialed. A kind nurse answered, telling me that Trish had suffered a broken arm and bruised ribs, and had some breathing issues, but was resting quietly. She was being administered pain medication, and they would know by morning if she would need surgery to have her spleen removed. And yes, I could visit her first thing in the morning.

I slept fitfully, tortured by one of my recurring nightmares. I thought of it as the chase dream. The setting of this dream changed but always involved me running from my father, along with my brothers and sisters. Dad is angry and screaming. We kids find a place to hide, usually under a bridge. As he walks across the bridge, I am terrified that one of the little ones will sneeze or cough, giving us away – but he walks right on by, and we escape.

The next morning, I skipped school and walked to Kaiser Hospital. I dreaded entering the pediatric ward, sure that a frightened little girl would beg me to take her home.

Trish shared a large hospital room with three other tiny occupants, all of them in crib-like beds with bars. Within each bed rose a mound of stuffed animals. The walls were brightly painted, and toys were stacked throughout the ward. I spotted Trish. She had tubes attached to her arms and nose. There was no mistaking those huge, expressive blue eyes and that blond hair, but I was not prepared for the look on her face. She was smiling!

A nurse told me that my sister would not need her spleen removed and that she was free to eat whatever she chose. I watched as another nurse served Trish a big bowl of ice cream. Several staff members checked on her during my visit, taking her vitals and asking how her pain was. She was cooed over and given plenty of attention. I imagined what a treat all of this must be for my sister, who had been only eleven months old when Bernadine was born into a household with eight other children.

Ten days later, when Patricia was due to be discharged, she cried and told the nurses that she wanted to *live* at the hospital. I knew how she must have felt. Her short life had been filled with nothing but trauma.

It pleased me to learn that my parents had taken shifts being with Trish, though I never bumped into either one during my daily visits. I'd felt reasonably sure that I wouldn't, as long as I visited the hospital at around 5:00 when the chaos of dinnertime at the McCusker household would prevent them from going anywhere.

Again, it struck me that any time my family was in my life, my comfortable and peaceful world would be shattered by the weight of their troubles. It felt impossible to sort through their burdens without taking them on as my own. When they were not around, my life felt worry-free, even though my family was always in my thoughts. Which was worse, I wondered – knowing the details, or imagining them? I addressed this topic frequently in my daily journaling, though I primarily wrote about Thom. In and out of my family's turmoil, I grounded myself in my relationship with him.

Though it was March, I was focused on May. Not only would I celebrate my eighteenth birthday but Thom was due to move to Hayward, following his discharge from the Navy. First and foremost, I wanted to look beautiful for him, so I began to jog every night after a lean dinner, and lost fifteen pounds.

Thom sent me money so I could find an apartment for him. I found an inexpensive furnished place on Harder Road in Hayward. Lost in a fantasy of how, one romantic evening, I would offer myself to him, I began to prepare. My first purchase was bed linen, then candles. I stowed a nightie in his closet and prepped the bathroom with two new toothbrushes, toothpaste, and scented soap.

I had yet to start my period, which had worried me over the past few years. I didn't feel like a woman yet. How I longed to join the ranks of my peers who complained about cramps and took Midol once a month. I wanted my boobs to grow and have a big mound of pubic hair.

After my surgery at age thirteen, I had been left with only one-fourth of a left ovary, and no right fallopian tube or ovary. I wondered if I had been left sterile, and would never even menstruate. This was not the sort of topic I could speak with Mrs. Donohue about. I recalled the surgeon up in Oakland reassuring me that my reduced left ovary would do the job of two full ovaries. But had he been humoring me? Were they allowed to do that? I had been told to take hormones for a month after that surgery, but my parents had not been able to afford the prescription. Had *that* caused my delayed period?

Unsure of what to do, I called Mrs. Etrium to ask if she could recommend a physician. I expressed my concern about being the only seventeen-year-old I knew who had not started her period, and confessed that I might soon be sexually active. If my surgery hadn't left me sterile, I would need to consider birth control options. How ideal to have this conversation over the phone so that she could not see me blush!

As I'd hoped, Mrs. Etrium responded to my concerns with understanding and support, as opposed to the judgment they might have been met within some circles – and to my grateful astonishment, she didn't even ask about my family or their whereabouts. She made arrangements for me to visit a Planned Parenthood clinic in Oakland and even drove me there.

As a result of that appointment, I started taking birth control pills. Twenty-eight days later, I had my first period. Only then did it occur to me to that it had *not* crossed my mind to discuss any of this with, or seek any advice from, my mother.

For some time, I had gradually become conscious of a new and different feeling about my mother. She had begun to seem like one of my helpless siblings, someone I needed to rescue and take care of.

It wasn't long before my mother even became a character in my chase dreams. Sometimes she was hiding under that bridge, right along with her children.

Chapter 24:

CLOSER TO HOME?

By the time Senior Ball rolled around, Thom was still at sea, so Pam and I went with a couple of nice, trustworthy sailors from NAS Alameda. I was so proud to stand in the reception line as a class officer and wished Thom could have been there to witness that small claim to fame. Our event committee had booked the Claremont Hotel in Berkeley – the fanciest place I'd ever set foot in, as it turned out – and tried to get Tower of Power to perform, but that group had a previous engagement. In 1969, though, the Bay area was bursting with quality musical acts, and our committee brought in a band called Cold Blood. Several of my classmates had heard them play at Fillmore West in the City, and we were thrilled to have them at our celebration.

I was not interested in joining any of the after-parties, so Pam and I returned to her house. I did want to visit Thom's apartment, though, so I drove one of the family cars up there, mainly intending to leave my corsage in his empty refrigerator.

I felt so grown up, turning the key in the lock and sauntering in, dreaming about how handsome Thom would have looked in a tuxedo, regretting more than ever not having had him as my escort. In a few weeks, I told myself, he would be home.

This was my third time in his apartment. While the place had come furnished, most of the furniture was cheap and tattered, so we had bought a lovely Mediterranean-style bedroom set before Thom shipped out. I'd added bed linen and a brown-and-gold comforter. The effect was irresistible, so I pulled down the sheets and comforter, puffed the brand-new pillows, and sat on the edge of the bed, kicking off my uncomfortable shoes.

I stripped off my evening gown and crawled into the bed wearing only my bra and panties, wondering what side Thom preferred. Having gotten there first, I claimed the left side. Struck by a sudden inspiration, I hopped out of bed and grabbed my clutch bag from the living room. Inside was a small bottle of Heaven Sent perfume. I sprinkled some on my side of the bed, and for good measure, splashed a bit on Thom's side. I looked around the room, imagining that this place could one day be my home. I was surprised to feel teary-eyed at the thought. It had been so long since I had felt the comfort of being completely at ease where I lived.

At that moment, I heard a sudden banging noise from below Thom's apartment. Rhythmic pounding, then silence, then more of the same. And voices, clearly audible from Thom's side of the bed. *Oh, no . . . loud neighbors.*

Looking toward the site of the commotion, I noticed a feeble ray of light shining up from below. Getting down on my hands and knees, I found a hole in the flooring, perhaps an inch in diameter. Peering through, I could make out two figures in a bed – and realized that they were a couple making love! I shifted from my right eye to my left several times. Clearly, I should not have been watching this, but I could not tear myself away.

Then, suddenly, it went dark below. They must have switched off a light. Muscle by muscle I slowly stood up, feeling my pantyhose snag on a splinter as I did. I crept to the bathroom, conscious now that the people below could probably hear me walking around, and found that I had a huge run in my stockings.

After plugging the peephole with toilet paper, I decided to buy a throw rug to go over it, and vowed never to look again, or tell anyone about my voyeurism. Then I got dressed and went back to the Donohue's.

The next few weeks were busy – graduation practice, cap-and-gown measurements, cutting school just for the naughtiness of it, and finally my *eighteenth birthday*. That birthday celebration ended up being the best of my young life. In my family, such things had always been limited by the unpredictability of our finances.

This time, Pam, Terri, and Gail – my three closest friends – took me out to dinner and, at the end, presented me with a special gift: a class ring! I'd given up on ordering one, as the price was prohibitive. But my friends had each chipped in one-third. They'd even had my initials engraved on the inside. It fit perfectly. "Thank you, my friends," I said, through eyes blurry with tears. After hugs and more tears, I left their company feeling so grateful.

When Pam and I arrived home, I was still giddy with delight. Mr. and Mrs. Donohue were watching television, and I bolted first to Mr. Donohue, telling him, "Look what I got for my birthday!" He smiled and took my hand as he investigated the ring, then asked his wife to take a look.

"What is it?" asked Mrs. Donohue.

"My senior class ring!" I said.

Without so much as a glance, she said, "One of these days, someone is going to come along and knock you off your high horse, girl."

Quickly Pam chimed in, "Mother! Why would you say that?"

Looking at my ring, bewildered, I blurted out, "What do you mean?"

She did not respond and just sat there, staring expressionlessly at the television. Utterly deflated, I found myself gripped by that old feeling from childhood. *I am not important, I am not safe, and I do not know where to hide.* I retreated to the bedroom to collect myself.

Within minutes came a knock on the door. I opened it to find Mr. Donohue, who said, "Time for your cake, Annie Roonie. Mrs. Donohue made it for you."

Several days before, Mrs. Donohue had asked me what my favorite cake was. "Vanilla with lemon filling, vanilla frosting, and sprinkles," I had told her.

By the time I ventured out to the dining room, the family had gathered there. I saw that the cake was chocolate, with chocolate frosting – Pam's favorite. Mr. Donohue lit the candles and they all sang a jolly round of Happy Birthday. I made my wish. *I need to feel at home some place.*

"Thank you so much, Mrs. Donohue! The cake is delicious," I said dutifully.

Even though it was the wrong kind of cake, this simple ceremony in the Donohue kitchen did restore some of my birthday gaiety. The thought that Thom would be back in a few days finished the job.

As the hour of his return drew near, I became more and more of a basket case. It was at least a fourteen-hour drive from Oak Harbor, Washington to Hayward, California, so Thom planned on leaving the day before and pulling over to sleep if needed. He hoped to be at the Donohue home sometime in the early afternoon. I'd showered the night before, and Pam set my hair in rollers. I'd arranged an afternoon off from NAS Alameda, so after one hour at school, I walked home.

This was a stupid mistake. All I could do was pace the house and check my appearance every fifteen minutes in the bathroom mirror (I was so pleased that I'd finished my period a week before, and that my complexion was clear). I tried reading, then listening to music, but ultimately ended up just staring out the front window. I rehearsed what I would say to Thom with Penny, the old Beagle whom I'd come to adore.

"Penny, what do you think? Should I be casual, and ask him how his trip was? Or should I grab him and plant a big kiss on his lips?" Penny just wagged her tail at each suggestion . . . well-meaning, but useless.

When Thom finally drove up in a dilapidated old black car, I ran outside, arms wide open. Thom made it easy. After hugging, kissing and a few minutes of catching up, he said, "Well, my lady, how about showing me my new residence?" He bowed with a sweeping gesture. God, how I loved this guy!

During our first hour back in his new apartment, Thom focused on setting up the new eight-track player, which he had bought in Japan. But then we adjourned to the bedroom, where Thom sniffed the scented air, grinned, and pulled me to him as we flopped onto the bed. Reluctantly, I untangled my body from his, smoothed my wrinkled clothing, and reminded him that the Donohues would be waiting for us.

We barely made it back in time for dinner that evening. Mrs. Donohue had asked us not to be late, as she had a surprise for Thom.

Upon Thom's plate at the dinner table rested a legal-sized envelope with his name written on it. Embossed in the upper-left corner, instead of a return address, were the words Caterpillar Tractor Company – Mrs. Donohue's employer; she worked production at their nearby plant.

She grinned at Thom, and said, "Go ahead, open the envelope. It's your surprise."

Thom tore it open to see VETERAN written in bold red across the top of a notice describing a job posting. Caterpillar gave preference to veterans, a policy developed after World War II.

"I put in a good word for you, Thom. I imagine you could have a job there if you're interested," said Mrs. Donohue.

I was glad that Thom had so easily won Mrs. Donohue's affections . . . and yet, I had to force myself to smile. Maybe I was a tad bit jealous. The longer I lived with the family, the more I felt that the matriarch was not very impressed with me. Still, even that could not disrupt my joy for any length of time, as long as I had Thom.

Thom jumped up to hug her. "Yes, ma'am! I would appreciate that!"

"This one is on swing shift, so you could go to school during the day. Ann Marie is off to Cal State, and Pam is going to Chabot Community College. College might be a good choice for you as well. You get your GI Bill, right?"

Frankly, I'd spent little time wondering how we would live once June arrived and I graduated from high school, so this offer of a good job struck me as unexpectedly timely and meaningful. Even so, Thom and I had other things on our minds that evening.

We rushed through dinner, anxious to return to his apartment. Moments after opening the door, we had already fallen into each other's arms. After a half hour of making out to Simon & Garfunkel, it felt like that moment of intimacy was dangerously close, so I whispered, "I don't think I'm ready." Later, we would share a laugh about that moment, when we discovered that he thought I was talking about a physical issue, while I was thinking about it in emotional terms.

Still, I did not resist when he carried me off to the bedroom and made love to me. Simon & Garfunkel were singing '*Scarborough Fair.*' I will never forget the special meaning that song holds for me now. Nor will I forget Thom's gentle touch, his tenderness, how natural it felt to be bonded to him.

We rested in one another's arms, as Thom stroked my face. *Can a wish really come to be so quickly? Can I dream of trusting myself, or him?* But I knew that I felt at home.

Having a midnight curfew, I managed to make it back before the enchanted hour, and quietly went to the bathroom. As I entered our bedroom, Pam shined a flashlight into the air.

"Can you please turn that thing off, Pam?"

"How was your evening?"

"The most wonderful of my entire life!"

"Did you do it? I mean, did you make love?" she asked.

"Yes, we did!" I said as I flopped onto my bed – but in that moment, I just wanted to be alone, and not share details. I wanted to relish and replay in my mind. But I knew that Pam wanted more, so we talked a bit, although I don't remember much about what I said. She seemed worried as if I had been violated in some way. Normally, I felt comforted by Pam's fierce sense of protection and loyalty for me. But not that night.

The next morning, there was a small package on the kitchen table, with a note from Mrs. Donohue. "Found this on the front porch this morning. Looks like it's from Thom." I ripped opened the manila envelope and found a cassette tape. I excused myself and went to our room, where I got out the cassette player. Thankfully, Pam did not follow me.

On the tape was a song *Morning Girl*, released the month before by a band called The Neon Philharmonic. The sound was not premium, as if Thom had taped it from the radio, but I recognized it immediately. Such a sweet tune, at number seventeen on the charts that month. As a gesture of love from Thom, it made number one with me.

School that day felt surreal. How could I go about my day as if everything was normal when I harbored such a special secret? Did it show on my face? I couldn't stop smiling, that's for sure.

Between classes, Pam passed me a long note. It was filled with affection, but there was something about it that annoyed me, something that I couldn't quite put my finger on. Maybe I wanted to enjoy my entry into womanhood more privately. But most of all, I just wanted to be with Thom.

Chapter 25:

COMMENCEMENT

My graduation ceremony was of little importance to me, save for what I hoped would happen once it was over. Assuming that at least a few of my family members would be present, I planned to introduce them to Thom.

Although there was always the chance that my family would show up looking less than presentable, or that my Dad would say something weird, this felt like the ideal environment for an introduction – it could be short and sweet, and Thom wouldn't see their house. And so, I paid very little attention to the ceremony and sat there obsessively twisting my tassel and scanning the audience. I picked Thom and the Donohue family out of the crowd but saw no sign of any McCuskers.

After the ceremony, Thom and I mingled for a while with friends and peers. We continued to hang back as the quad gradually emptied out, just in case. But the crowd went on thinning with no McCuskers in sight, and the Donohue family drove home. Once the quad was almost empty, Thom and I walked back to the Donohue's. *OK*, I told myself, *I made the effort.*

Mom called me from a payphone later that evening, with the news that Dad had been arrested earlier that very day.

"He wanted to see you graduate, Annie Girl, and he wanted the kids to be there. He was so proud of you! He figured we could drive the four miles in that stolen car. It's been sitting in the garage for months. He put the Arizona plates back on. They handcuffed him right in Mount Eden's parking lot, in front of the kids!"

"Where is he now, Mama?"

231

"In jail!" she wailed, followed by uncontrollable weeping.

"I'll try to get right over. See you in about forty-five minutes, if I have to walk."

Glad that Thom had already gone back to his apartment, I confided in Pam. Also very glad that we were now eighteen years old, and that Pam had unlimited use of her brother's car. All we had to tell Pam's parents was, "See you in a couple of hours", and out the door we went.

The sight, which greeted us at the apartment on Chisholm Court, brought on a flashback of Snedigar Cottage. All of my siblings sat on the couch or on the floor, solemn and waiting . . . so much like that morning of the court hearing, where their family's future was to be determined by strangers. While my siblings sat as still as stones, Mom ran to my arms and filled me in on what had happened.

Dad had run into a drinking buddy, in whom he had confided, for reasons unknown, about the stolen car. After the two of them had gotten into a drunken altercation, the guy had snitched my dad out. Dad was being held in Hayward's small jail, at least until his arraignment on Monday. Until then, we would know nothing, unless someone posted the five-hundred-dollar bail.

I handed Pam a five-dollar-bill, asking if she could please dash to the store and buy a half-gallon of Neapolitan ice cream, and get most of the change in dimes. As she left to run that errand, I walked slowly toward my siblings, patting my knees and looking at the little ones. I was barely seated on the floor before Trish and Bernadine had perched on my lap. Billy and Rosemary took positions on either side of me, putting their heads on my shoulders. We all sat there silently until Pam returned. There was no need for words; we'd all been here many times before. Fear and uncertainty had been frequent guests at the McCusker household.

And then Pam was back, chirping, "Ice cream, anyone?" as she walked in.

The spell broken, all seven siblings dashed into the kitchen, where I sliced the ice cream into even slabs and served them on plates. Midway through this happy task, I suddenly recognized the knife I was using – but managed to press on and maintain an upbeat demeanor.

I considered taking this opportunity to spend the night. But then I remembered that Thom and I were going to . . . *Thom! Oh my God, what am I going to tell Thom about all of this?*

I handed over the change to my Mom, saying, "Here's a bunch of dimes, so you can call the jail, and call me. We'll take the bus the day after tomorrow to go to court." Then to my brother Tom, I said, "You okay watching the kids?"

"Yeah, sure," he replied.

I took at quick look through the cupboards and refrigerator. They had food, but I would need to borrow twenty bucks from Thom for additional groceries. After many hugs, Pam and I headed home.

Thom had saved enough money that he didn't need to start at Caterpillar until mid-July. We had time to play together and we became inseparable. Since I was eighteen, the Donohues lifted my midnight curfew, but I had to be home and in bed before they left for work in the morning.

If Pam felt left out, she never let on. Still, Thom and I made every effort to include her in our activities, and she did likewise. Pam's interest in Special Education led her to start work with a teacher in the field, and so our threesome began volunteering in a group home for 'mentally retarded' boys. Once a month, we took the boys out for a picnic lunch in the park.

Thom, Pam, and I also started a regular backpacking group with some of our fellow volunteers. Using mostly borrowed equipment, we ventured out into the wilds of northern California; our longest stretch, amongst the Redwoods, lasted for five days. On the last night of that trip, Thom and I invited Pam to join us in our tent. With me squeezed into the middle, we ate crackers with peanut butter and laughed until it grew dark. Thom could be hysterically funny, particularly when he donned his Tennessee accent and imitated a brainless hick.

A guy I'd met in karate class worked in a dive shop. We invited him over to the apartment for dinner, along with Pam. Before long the three of us were in the Pacific Ocean, working on our scuba certification. Bart would "borrow" equipment from the shack in the evenings, and off we'd go to Lover's Point in Monterrey Bay the next day. The freebies ended when it became clear that Pam had no interest in Bart, but shortly thereafter, we all earned certification and could get our own tanks filled.

All of this physical activity felt wonderful, as I'd had little exercise since quitting karate halfway through my senior year. What a memorable, fun time in my life – save for that gnawing worry that was always in the back of my mind, occasionally dormant but sometimes fierce.

It took me a week to tell Thom the whole story about my father's arrest, sharing details a few at a time. I would study his face as I spoke, searching for signs of shock, disgust, or God forbid, judgment of me. And each time, he cupped my face in his hands and told me that he was marrying me, not my family. His reassurance was helpful – and almost believable. But really, how could he not wonder if this troubled-family malaise had not rubbed off on me?

Only once, and ever so gently, did he suggest that I consider disassociating myself from them. *Like cutting off my right arm*, I thought. *Completely impossible. They need me. I have to be there for them.* What I said out loud was, "Maybe someday, but it doesn't feel like the right time."

Dad was ultimately sentenced to thirty days in jail. Since he was the sole breadwinner for a large family, he was permitted to serve his sentence during his two days off each week – five days home, then two in jail. Alameda County's Santa Rita jail was in Dublin, about twelve miles from Hayward. Mom took him there and picked him up, so she would have the use of his demo car during his absence. She was a terrible driver, having had little experience, so I went along when I could, Dad driving there and me driving back. The jail creeped me out. It was huge and looked like a full-blown prison. Thom offered to help with transportation, but I wanted him to have no part in this. That would only cause me more shame and humiliation.

It became more and more difficult to leave our apartment each night, after the closeness that our lovemaking brought. It didn't occur to me to just move in with Thom; it was a given that I would remain with the Donohue family until married. So, spurred on by our reluctance to be apart, we set a wedding date: November 8, 1969.

One day, Thom said to me, "Well, it's time to meet your family, soon-to-be Mrs. Walker. I've been here for a month and a half, Ann Marie. There's no more putting it off. Let's go tell them that we're getting hitched."

He finished this ultimatum with a huge grin. How could I say no to that? Unable to further delay this inevitable meeting, we set a second date: Monday, July 7, a day my dad would be home.

On Tuesday, July 1, I stopped by the apartment on Chisholm Court to let Mom know I'd be bringing Thom by to meet the family in six days, and that we had a surprise to share.

My initial plan was to visit Chisolm Court again on the 6th. I would tidy the place up, and take some clothes to the laundromat, ensuring the kids had something clean to wear. Oh, and I could bring some soda and chips and French Onion soup dip to serve. Yes, and I needed to be sure the ice cube trays were full.

But then I remembered that several of us had planned a backpacking trip over the Independence Day holiday, leaving on the 3rd and returning on the 6th. Thom was just going to have to meet them, sans any preparation on my part. And my fretting continued . . .

Monday was a gorgeous day in Hayward, so Thom and I decided to walk from his place on Harder Road to Chisholm Court. We spent the entire time discussing what he could expect. A few blocks from our destination, we bought soda, chips, dip, and a bag of candy at a Safeway. Heading onward with our groceries, with just minutes to go until the big moment, my fretting reached a boiling point.

"Remember, they don't have a washer and dryer, so it's hard for Mom to get to the laundromat." And further, "Mom tries to keep the place tidy, but it's difficult with so many kids in such a small place." And finally, "Remember, if Dad is drinking . . . "

"I know, I know!" Thom interrupted. He stopped dead in his tracks and sat the grocery bag on the ground. He faced me and took me gently by the shoulders. Could he feel my anxious breathing, my racing heart?

"We leave after fifteen minutes if he is drinking," Thom said firmly. Then his voice became softer as he continued, "When are you going to settle down and realize that I don't give a hoot about your family background?" He took my hand and looked at me as though actually expecting an answer.

"Well sailor, possibly about an hour from now." I grinned and kissed him.

Spotting the apartment complex, I thought for the dozenth time how much it resembled a motel. An outside stairway led to the second floor, a long row of identical doors and windows. I paused after a few steps up to look across at the adjacent lot, where a twin apartment building was under construction, only the foundations and framing complete. Each day at five o'clock the work over there ended, and it had become a favorite place for the little ones to play in the evenings.

A few visits back, I found Trish and Bernadine constructing a dollhouse from small, discarded pieces of wood. They'd used rocks and clumps of dirt to furnish their creation, and even had a line of nails forming a walkway to the front door. The little ones had taken a couple of Billy's green plastic soldiers and posted one of each side of the rock door. How I wished they were there now, so I could show off their cute and imaginative work – perhaps even break the ice by having Thom meet them first.

But they were not there, and we continued up the stairs, heading for #6. At the door, I started our family's secret knock, when the door swung open on its hinges. Thom gave me a puzzled look . . . but I immediately and instinctively *knew*.

Inside, the place was a wreck, clothing strewn everywhere, a sense of absence so heavy in the air that it was palpable.

I turned to Thom, and said, "They're gone."

Epilogue

I was to learn later that after skipping California in 1969, my family moved to Gresham, Oregon. The reason? My father had no longer wished to serve his jail time. Simple as that.

Thom met my family eight months after we married. Several of his Navy cronies lived up in Washington State, and Gresham was on the way there. After nearly a year of hand-wringing on my part, the visit turned out to be blissfully uneventful. Thom even told me afterward that he found my father "likable."

I learned from my siblings that Dad's violent behavior had ceased. The fact that Tom, Ed, and Jim had by then grown into physically imposing teenagers probably had something to do with that.

By 1973, I'd finished my Master of Science degree and worked as a seventh-grade counselor in the Bay Area. I visited my family again during spring break of 1974, while in Oregon for a job interview at Linn-Benton Community College in Albany.

It remains a mystery to me why I was chosen over two hundred seventy-six other applicants for that position. But thankfully, I was. I moved to the beautiful Pacific Northwest and spent the rest of my professional career as a counselor at LBCC.

One day, many years into my community college experience, something on a colleague's bulletin board caught my eye as I walked into her office. Amongst the notices and papers, sayings, and photos pinned up there, I noticed a small yellow post-it. In her own hand, my colleague had written, "There is no fixing a damaged childhood; the best you can do is make the sucker float."

Perhaps too true. And this saying, which I later learned came from Pat Conroy's novel <u>The Prince of Tides</u>, has stayed with me through the intervening years. It became one of several converging inspirations, which triggered the writing of this memoir.

I have come to believe that my own struggle with poverty, and the ills which so often accompany it, has helped me to better understand the struggles of others. This hard-won insight became a pillar of my professional life. And now, although it has often been difficult to describe the events chronicled in this book, I hope that in my tale of growth, perseverance, and triumph over adversity – along with the fumbling, doubt, and heartache, which come with every life's journey – readers may find inspiration. Sometimes, the only way Home is the longest.

About the Author

Ann Marie Etheridge earned her Master of Science degree in Counseling Psychology and spent her professional career on the faculty of a community college. Within a short time, it was obvious that Ann Marie had the skill and propensity to work with folks who came from "the other side of the tracks," as she did.

Ann Marie has published professionally in the American Psychologist journal. *Long Way Home* is her first book. Ann Marie lives in Corvallis, Oregon.

Made in the USA
San Bernardino, CA
31 August 2018